TAKEOVER

TAKEOVER

EXPLAINING THE EXTRAORDINARY RISE OF THE SNP

Rob Johns & **James Mitchell**

Biteback Publishing

First published in Great Britain in 2016 by
Biteback Publishing Ltd
Westminster Tower
3 Albert Embankment
London SE1 7SP

ISBN 978-1-78590-032-7

10 9 8 7 6 5 4 3 2 1

A CIP catalogue record for this book is available from the British Library.

Set in Sabon and Bell Gothic by Adrian McLaughlin

Printed and bound in Great Britain by
CPI Group (UK) Ltd, Croydon CR0 4YY

MIX
Paper from
responsible sources
FSC® C020471

CONTENTS

PREFACE

It is September 2013, a year before the Scottish independence referendum. The polls are static, with 'Yes' languishing. US polling guru Nate Silver has declared that there is 'virtually no chance' of a vote for independence, and the newspapers are mulling over the consequences of a resounding 'No' vote. A punter walks into a bookmaker and places a £10 treble on the following sequence of events: there will be a 45 per cent vote for independence in the referendum; turnout will be 85 per cent; and, within a year of that vote, the SNP would hold all but three of Scotland's seats in the House of Commons. The bookmaker puts the ten-pound note in the till with an amused shake of the head, hoping to see plenty more of that customer.

That bet is just a fantasy. Certainly neither of us placed it. We do not pretend to have foreseen these extraordinary developments. But we hope in this book to have gone some way towards explaining them. Many readers, both north and south of the border, will have looked on in puzzlement as well as surprise at the recent electoral goings-on in Scotland. This book is aimed at them and at helping to resolve at least some of that puzzlement.

The analysis that follows is based on reflections on much of our previous and ongoing research. We have returned to studies of previous Scottish and UK elections, mainly funded by the Economic and Social Research Council (ESRC), as well as drawing on other work conducted by colleagues across a number of universities. Research on the Scottish referendum, also funded by the ESRC, conducted with Ailsa Henderson and Chris Carman, has also made a major contribution to this study. Finally, anyone researching Scottish public opinion is much obliged to the Scottish Centre for Social Research for its outstanding What Scotland Thinks website. This has exponentially reduced the time required to find opinion polls, to track attitudes over time, and to check those boring methodological details that we have tried to spare readers of this book but which need to be out there somewhere.

The book analyses not only shifts in public opinion but also the internal politics of the SNP. Our 2007–9 study of the SNP's membership, undertaken along with Lynn Bennie and again funded by the ESRC, helped us to understand that party at a critical juncture in its history after it came to power for the first time in 2007. We have also benefited from access to data that the SNP has collected on its new members, which helped to inform our developing understanding of these changes, and we thank the party for their willingness to share this information with us.

We would want to pay particular thanks to colleagues with whom we have worked over the years. We have been following and discussing Scottish politics for many years, discussing developments with friends, colleagues and countless acquaintances along the way. We worked together for some time at Strathclyde University and gained from the support of friends and colleagues there and much of this book draws on work started then. It would be difficult to list all those who have helped us and so here we confine ourselves to naming those busy friends and colleagues who offered comments on parts of the manuscript as it was in progress. We are very grateful for the helpful and insightful suggestions and corrections from Ewan Crawford of West of Scotland University and a former adviser to First Minister Salmond; Nicola McEwen of Edinburgh University; Colin Mackay of Scottish Television; and Kevin Adamson.

This book was therefore a collaborative exercise, nowhere more so than in the search for a title. One author's fondness for allusions to song lyrics left the other baffled (and then there is the additional problem that titles like 'It Was All Yellow' might leave unwelcome songs in readers' heads).

Having struggled to find a title that we both agreed on, let alone one that the publishers endorsed as well, we turned to Twitter to seek suggestions. This certainly lightened the hours spent working on the manuscript but it proved less enlightening when it came to the search for serious options. In the event, as readers will have seen, we opted for a straightforward rather than a startling title. But this provides a good opportunity to list some of the runners-up – from the relative subtlety of 'Conscious Uncoupling', 'No Means Yes' and 'Escape Velocity?' to the ingenious punning of 'Yes Wee Clan' and 'Jock and Awe' – and to acknowledge the creative efforts of Guy Browning, David Tuck, Adam Evans, Stair at the Sky, Christopher Dart, Chris Hanretty, Aaron Bell, Rob Ford, Michael Bone and many others.

From the title onward, of course, any errors of judgement, interpretation or fact are our responsibility. The developments discussed in this book are in many ways ongoing and doubtless our conclusions will be refined by subsequent events, results, surveys and conversations. Nonetheless, we expect that the main thrust of our argument will stand.

Last but not least, we are very grateful to our meticulous editors and proofreaders. This work was begun by Alec Johns, without whose scrutiny this book would have contained (even) more of the kind of long and turgid sentences – certainly containing and often beginning with subordinate clauses – of which this is an example. Then Olivia Beattie at Biteback Publishing did a superb job of making the argument clearer and stronger and the text more readable. Working with Biteback has opened our academic eyes to the notion that it need not take a minimum of two and a half years to take a book from conception to publication. Their efficiency has brought this idea to fruition sooner than we would have thought possible. We are grateful for that, as well as for their broader interest in and support for the project.

CHAPTER 1

FROM 6 TO 56

This is a story of electoral supremacy. Ten years ago, it would have been more or less unthinkable that a book about the SNP would be described thus. Since then, the party has not only overtaken its rivals in Scotland; it has reached the kind of electoral market share that is unheard of in modern British politics. The SNP won almost exactly half of the Scottish vote in the 2015 general election and took fifty-six of the fifty-nine seats at Westminster, leaving Scotland's electoral map a sea of yellow. Since then, as shown in Figure 1.1, the party has also consistently polled over 50 per cent in constituency vote intentions for the Scottish Parliament.

During half a century as Scotland's largest party, Labour never managed to break the 50 per cent barrier. No party has done so at the UK level since before the Second World War.

FIGURE 1.1: CONSTITUENCY VOTE INTENTION POLLS FOR
      THE 2016 SCOTTISH PARLIAMENT ELECTION,
      MAY 2015–APRIL 2016

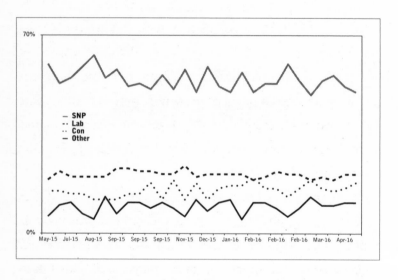

When the architects of devolution opted for a broadly proportional system, this was in part an insurance policy against the SNP winning a majority in Holyrood on the basis of a minority of votes. There was no way of insuring against the SNP winning a majority of *votes*. But then the notion would have been fanciful anyway. After all, it is not only in Britain that a 50 per cent vote share is a rarity. It has been achieved occasionally – by the Christian Social Union in Bavaria, for example, and the Social Democratic Party in Portugal – but these are very rare exceptions. And not even these parties soared to 50 per cent at the rate of the SNP. It might be objected that we are not comparing like with like here: the Scottish political system established by devolution is newer than those across Western Europe, and startling results – such as by Democratic Labour in Lithuania and by the Croatian Democratic Union, with their 45 per cent won in the early 1990s – are possible while such systems bed down. Yet the SNP's surge was not achieved in a new democracy as such, nor in the first couple of elections before its vote share settled back down as a new electoral and party system became established. It is exactly as devolved government and politics in Scotland become more ordinary that the election results are becoming extraordinary.

While the SNP's Holyrood and Westminster vote shares now look very similar at around 50 per cent, this convergence is new. Previously, and for the obvious reason that the SNP is a much more significant player in Scottish than in UK general elections, the party has polled more heavily in the former. Moreover, its projected 2016 showing marks only a relatively small increase on the previous Scottish Parliament election. The SNP's majority in that 2011 contest was not just one of a series of seismic electoral shocks in Scotland; it was also a pre-condition of what followed in the 2014 referendum and the 2015 general election. Given this importance, we devote three chapters (Chapters 3–5) of this book to understanding how the party achieved electoral predominance at Holyrood. This chapter, however, is about the SNP at Westminster, and about how the party went from six to fifty-six Scottish seats in five years.

THE LONG VIEW

Table 1.1 records the SNP's performance in every UK general election since 1945. The early post-war years were not a success. Performance was as much about how many candidates the party was able to get onto the ballot, and how many of these retained their deposit, as it was about winning votes. Given that the party is estimated to have had only around 200 members in the late 1950s, it is not surprising that they struggled to raise more than a handful of deposits. In 1955, the SNP came close to having no candidates at all when the only person nominated threatened to withdraw if no other candidate emerged. This obviously limited the party's electoral potential. Of course, there is a 'Which came first?' issue here: the lack of members and candidates is not just a cause but also a consequence of limited public appetite for Scottish nationalism. Nonetheless, the fact that SNP candidates often polled quite well where they did compete suggests that there was at least some such appetite. Even given that the party would naturally stand first in the most propitious territory, there are signs that the problem lay in the supply of as well as the demand for candidates. Between 1955 and 1970 the

SNP more or less doubled its Scottish vote share at every election but largely through a similar doubling in the number of seats in which it stood. It's not that the average candidate was doing better – there were just a lot more of them.

TABLE 1.1: SNP CANDIDATES AND PERFORMANCE
IN POST-WAR GENERAL ELECTIONS

ELECTION	CANDIDATES	% DEPOSITS RETAINED	% SCOTTISH VOTE	MEAN % IN SEATS FOUGHT	SEATS	% SEATS	% SEATS - % VOTES
1945	8	25	1.2	9.4	0	0	-1.2
1950	3	0	0.4	7.4	0	0	-0.4
1951	2	50	0.3	19.9	0	0	-0.3
1955	2	50	0.5	14.7	0	0	-0.5
1959	5	40	0.8	11.3	0	0	-0.8
1964	15	20	2.4	10.6	0	0	-2.4
1966	23	33	5.0	14.1	0	0	-5.0
1970	65	43	11.4	12.8	1	1.4	-10.0
1974 Feb	70	90	21.9	22.1	7	9.7	-12.2
1974 Oct	71	100	30.4	30.4	11	15.3	-15.1
1979	71	59	17.3	17.3	2	2.8	-14.5
1983	72	26	11.8	11.8	2	2.8	-9.0
1987	71	99	14.0	14.1	3	4.2	-9.8
1992	72	100	21.5	21.5	3	4.2	-17.3
1997	72	100	21.9	21.9	6	8.3	-13.6
2001	72	100	21.1	21.1	5	6.9	-14.2
2005	59	100	17.7	17.7	6	10.2	-7.5
2010	59	100	19.9	19.9	6	10.2	-9.7
2015	59	100	50.0	50.0	56	94.9	+44.9

When the SNP's Winnie Ewing famously won the Hamilton by-election in 1967, this was a surprise but not a bolt from the blue to those who had noted the steady progress made in general elections, other by-elections and local council contests. Nonetheless, it proved a turning point in terms of media interest and publicity, and can be said to be the point at which the SNP ceased to be a fringe party in Scottish politics. Thereafter it always polled above 10 per cent and always won at least one seat in Westminster elections. In 1970, Ewing lost Hamilton back to Labour but Donald Stewart in the Western Isles – the very last seat to declare – was eventually announced as the SNP's first general election victor.

It was in the two elections of 1974 that, in the eyes of the two major parties, the SNP moved from being an irritant to posing a serious threat. The 30.4 per cent achieved in the October contest, building on the 22 per cent won eight months before, is still a long way short of 50 per cent but nonetheless represents a very strong showing at a Westminster election and its best result until 2015. And the contrast between October 1974 and May 2015 is exaggerated by the electoral system. A 20 percentage point difference in vote share means an 80 percentage point difference in seat share. As all the negative numbers in the rightmost column of Table 1.1 show, the SNP had been a serial sufferer at the hands of first-past-the-post, its vote being distributed relatively evenly across Scotland. However, there are tipping points in the Westminster electoral system, at which a small increase in vote share causes a sudden rush of seats. Even if no one was foreseeing anything like the near-clean sweep of 2015, there was widespread acknowledgement in 1974 that the SNP was close to such a tipping point. At the October election, the party held only seven seats but was in second place in fifteen more. An SNP vote just a few points higher than its 30 per cent in October 1974 would have brought major seat dividends.

So 2015 did not quite come out of nowhere. October 1974 shows that, if the conditions are right, polling heavily in UK general elections has long been within the SNP's scope. The question is: what are those conditions? We suggest that there are three. First, something has to make the 'Scottish question' relevant – that is, to highlight a divergence of interests between Scotland and the rest of the UK and, by implication, the advantages of self-government. Second, the election outcome at the UK level has to be perceived as being in the balance between the two major parties. Third, the SNP already has to be seen as a relevant or viable electoral force in Scotland. The first condition provides the impetus to *consider* the SNP; the second and third conditions are about persuading voters that this would not be a wasted vote.

October 1974 illustrates all three conditions very clearly. Admittedly, the widespread notion that the SNP was carried to 30.4 per cent purely on a tide of North Sea oil is simplistic. Smaller parties were gaining at the expense of the major forces elsewhere in the UK – indeed, all over Western

Europe – and so there are reasons to suppose that the SNP would have won ground anyway. But oilfields were being discovered in the North Sea from the late 1960s, opening up a bonanza in tax revenues, and this became the lubricant enabling the party to take particular advantage of economic discontent and the wider trend of detachment from traditional party loyalties. Amid an economic crisis exacerbated by spiralling oil prices, the phrase 'It's Scotland's Oil' highlighted an unusually tangible benefit of independence. Indeed, according to Bill Miller's 1981 study of voting in the 1974 elections, the effect of oil was not to deliver temporary protest votes to the SNP from those who nonetheless remained staunchly Unionist. Rather, it triggered voters to reflect on the divergence of the interests of Scotland from those of the UK government. Such reflection made an SNP vote a likelier choice.

The outcome of the February 1974 election, when Labour became the largest party but short of a majority, meant that the October re-run fulfilled the second condition for SNP progress. It looked quite likely that once again no party would win an overall majority and it looked at least conceivable that the SNP would then hold the balance of power. There was a new ring of authenticity in the party's claim that, the larger the SNP group at Westminster, the greater the party's power to bargain in Scotland's interests. This made it doubly important that the party had already made a seats breakthrough in the February election. Talk of a powerful

SNP cohort would have sounded a little far-fetched had that cohort at the time still consisted only of Donald Stewart. This is the third condition in action: February 1974 had shown the SNP as a significant electoral player, and so by October it was harder than ever before for the party's opponents to play the 'wasted vote' card against it.

The first two conditions are to a large extent out of the SNP's hands. The discovery of North Sea oil, for example, was simply a trump card dealt into the party's 1974 hand. Of course, the party will seek a 'why this means Scotland needs independence' angle in whatever issues are prominent at a given election, but this is rarely as easy as in the case of oil. There is even less that the SNP can do about the likelihood of a hung parliament at Westminster. In 1979, for example, the constitutional question slipped well down the agenda following the unsuccessful devolution referendum four years earlier, refocusing Scottish attention on the battle between Labour and the Conservatives at the UK level. And the latter's majority was widely forecast, meaning that even an expanded cohort of SNP MPs would have nothing like the power that they enjoyed during the 1974–79 parliament.

When it comes to the third condition, however, the SNP does have some control. The party was in generally rude health in 1974 (see Miller, 1981, pp. 258–9). It was well-organised, united and widely seen – even by those opposed to independence – as fighting in Scotland's interests. Insofar as parties can make themselves more electorally presentable in this way, they can enhance their relevance. The flip side of this, of course, is that they can also undermine their relevance. And this is what happened after 1974 in particular and to some extent in subsequent Westminster elections. Admittedly, the electoral system bears some responsibility here. Even a successful election in terms of vote share would yield a meagre harvest of seats. The resulting sense of disappointment – often exacerbated by the raising of expectations by bombastic pre-election predictions – would aggravate existing divisions over strategy and direction, and this disunity would further weaken the party's credibility in advancing the same claim to relevance at the next election. Thus the SNP remained an oppositional and amateurish party, struggling to maintain a significant presence at Westminster – not only on the green benches but also in media coverage and public attention. While, as in 1974, circumstances sometimes conspired to give the SNP sudden relevance, the default situation was one in which the 'wasted vote' accusation would hit home.

A PERFECT STORM

In the previous section, we identified three ingredients for SNP success in Westminster elections. In all three cases, the party's cup was running over in 2015. First, although the referendum should theoretically have settled the constitutional question, in practice it did anything but. As we discuss in Chapter 7, a combination of the momentum that 'Yes' took from the campaign and the perceived importance of 'The Vow' of more powers for the Scottish Parliament meant that the Scottish dimension in general, and further devolution in particular, was very much relevant in 2015. In a February poll by TNS-BMRB, respondents were given a list of issues and asked to nominate such of these as would be 'very important to you when considering how you will vote' in the upcoming general election. Further devolution was chosen by 25 per cent and independence by 24 per cent of the respondents, and in each case the overwhelming majority also reported a vote intention for the SNP. On the face of it, 'more powers' – which throughout and beyond the referendum campaign was the average voter's favoured constitutional option – was a closer match with the Labour, Conservative and Liberal Democrat positions than that of the SNP. As in the 1970s, however, the British parties were not trusted to deliver these powers unless the SNP was there to 'hold their feet to the fire', to use Alex Salmond's phrase when he announced he was standing down as leader after the referendum. Four weeks before polling day in 2015, YouGov asked the following question: 'Thinking about the MPs elected from Scotland at the next general election, which party would be most effective at securing increased powers for the Scottish Parliament?' Of those who gave an answer, fully 75 per cent chose the SNP. Labour was second

with 15 per cent. 'None of them' finished ahead of the
Conservatives and Liberal Democrats. To the extent that voters were choosing based on constitutional matters in 2015,
the SNP stood to profit heftily.

However, and as usual in Scottish elections both to
Westminster and to Holyrood, voting specifically on the constitutional question is a minority pursuit (see, for example,
Johns et al., 2010, pp. 61–3). In that TNS-BMRB poll, both
of the constitutional issues trailed well behind health, education, jobs and pensions when respondents named the issues
important to them when they voted. And, as the first column in Table 1.2 shows, when British Election Study (BES)
respondents were asked during the election campaign about
what they saw as 'the single most important issue facing the
country at the present time', the constitution was not one of
the top concerns for Scottish voters. They were instead preoccupied with the same bread-and-butter issues on which
the election was fought throughout Britain.

This would normally have spelt trouble for the SNP by
focusing Scottish voters' minds on the choice between Labour
and the Conservatives as plausible options for governing the
UK. In 2015, however, there was plainly a Scottish dimension to most of these everyday concerns. Clear majorities
of those most concerned with poverty and inequality,
or the state and funding of public services, deemed the SNP
the best party to handle these, echoing the referendum campaign in which 'Yes' made much of these issues. Rather

than choosing *a* Westminster government, some voters seem still to have been reflecting on the perceived limitations *of* Westminster government.

TABLE 1.2: MOST IMPORTANT ISSUES AND PARTY BEST ABLE
TO HANDLE THEM, APRIL 2015

	% NAMING THAT ISSUE (COLUMN SUMS TO 100)	% NAMING PARTY AS BEST ABLE TO HANDLE THAT ISSUE (ROWS SUM TO 100)					
		CON	LAB	SNP	OTHER	NONE	N
Economy	34	42	15	23	4	16	1309
Immigration	14	15	8	9	49	18	519
Poverty/inequality	12	0	22	57	13	8	446
Public services	11	13	12	63	6	6	410
NHS	10	4	42	33	5	16	365
All others	20	16	14	34	15	21	751

Source: BESIP Scottish respondents, campaign wave

The strong SNP ratings in Table 1.2 partly reflect the changed status of Westminster elections following devolution. Like candidates and journalists, voters do not always respect constitutional boundaries when deciding what matters in an election. If they regard, say, education as the most pressing issue in the run-up to a UK general election, voters might reasonably declare the SNP as the best (or worst) party to handle that issue based on its performance in office at Holyrood. They might also – perhaps less reasonably but still understandably – go on to vote for (or against) the SNP in a Westminster election despite the devolved status of education. The SNP therefore stood to benefit in 2015 from what we will see in Chapter 5 were strongly positive evaluations of its record in Scottish government.

Yet there is more to this than the constitutional position. Macroeconomic policy remains reserved to Westminster (and the Bank of England). When 23 per cent of those who mentioned economic concerns then went on to name the SNP as best able to handle this issue, it is conceivable but improbable that they had Holyrood in mind as the party's main channel for doing so. More likely is that they saw, across a range of issues, scope for substantial Scottish influence at the UK level. The SNP was obviously not going to be leading the Westminster government but it might have plenty of say over its formation and its policies.

That brings us to the second condition for SNP success: a general election in the balance. Here, the party in 2015 owed a considerable debt to the opinion polls. The inquiry into the pollsters' collective failure has, at least in the preliminary conclusions available at the time of writing, put the blame squarely on consistently unrepresentative samples. There may have been a small late swing to the Conservatives, the inquiry concluded, but this made only a minor contribution to the major difference between the polling predictions and the election outcome. In short: the polls were wrong all along. Labour and the Conservatives were not neck-and-neck and the big question should have been whether the Conservatives would secure a majority, not whether they would edge out Labour as the largest party in a hung parliament. This hugely affected the dynamics of the campaign in general, and the SNP's place in particular.

Our main focus is on voting in Scotland, but it is worth highlighting one implication of this polling failure for what happened south of the border. If the polls were wrong all along, then the Conservative majority was not the direct consequence of a last-minute swing among voters fearful of a Labour minority government held to ransom by the SNP. This narrative had been prominent in Conservative campaigning since the beginning of the year and so may have contributed to what we now believe was its persistent lead. Nonetheless, when it comes to the short campaign, it is hard to reconcile the stability of the polling picture with the ramping up of rhetoric in the Tories' campaign and supportive media (including the posters and videos with Miliband either nestling in Sturgeon's and Salmond's breast pockets or dancing to their tunes). The fact that this failed to extend the Conservatives' lead suggests that that lead – and the eventual Conservative majority – was due instead to the party's clear advantages over Labour on key criteria like economic competence and leadership. Indeed, in their detailed analyses of individual voters' choices, the BES team report finding 'little robust evidence that attitudes towards the SNP and expectations about a hung parliament resulted in gains for the Conservatives' (BES, 2015). This may sound far-fetched to those involved in the ground campaigns, and there is no doubt that survey questions often fail to capture the essence of a pivotal message or issue. At the same time, those subscribing to the 'SNP fear' thesis may have mistaken correlation for causation. The fact that there was genuine public scepticism about the legitimacy of a Labour–SNP coalition – and that this would naturally come up on doorsteps given its prominence in campaigning and media coverage – does not mean that this swung votes or caused the eventual Conservative victory, the seeds of which were probably long sown.

Back to Scotland, and here things are much more clear-cut. Those same BES data confirm that, other things remaining the same, those who expected a hung parliament were more likely to vote SNP (BES, 2015). The widespread expectation of a hung parliament gave a major boost to a party whose post-election influence depended heavily – not entirely, but heavily – on neither the Conservatives nor Labour winning outright. Here, the images of Miliband, coalition scenarios, and parliamentary arithmetic probably mattered less than the simple equation proposed in one of the SNP's own posters: 'More SNP seats. More power for Scotland.' There is also a simple point about visibility. Even given its new-found dominance in the polls, the SNP is always in danger of being sidelined in a Westminster campaign. The Conservatives' preoccupation with the SNP, targeted at an English audience, helped give the party a starring role in Scottish election coverage that it would not otherwise have enjoyed. Just being talked about was useful to the SNP; being talked about as a pivotal player was doubly so.

The polls in 2010 also pointed (and this time more accurately) to a hung parliament. However, this seems to have been met with more scepticism. Certainly the 2010 campaign was less dominated, both in Scotland and the UK as a whole, by the question of likely post-election agreements and alliances. One likely reason is that, at that time, majorities were the norm. By 2015, however, there had been five years of a coalition government at Westminster. Hung parliaments no longer seemed either outlandish or unworkable, and the more apocalyptic predictions about the consequences of inconclusive elections had begun to sound faintly ridiculous. It is probably not a coincidence, then, that the SNP's two strongest Westminster performances to date have come in the elections *following* hung parliaments, and that its strongest performance followed a stable, full-term coalition government.

During the final eight weeks of the campaign, the BES asked: 'Which of these parties do you think has no real chance of being part of the next UK government?' In Figure 1.2, we show the percentages of Scottish and English respondents who named the SNP as one of those parties with no such chance of office, and how this changed over the campaign period. In fact, it did not change much in Scotland. Throughout March and April, only a small minority of around 15 per cent of Scots ruled the SNP out of government formation. The graph gives the impression of the English electorate, understandably less familiar with the SNP and its prospects, slowly catching up with the 'reality' of the polling situation. However, at no point does the English proportion dip below the Scottish. This is hard to square with the notion that the English electorate, following a campaign that became almost fixated with the post-election shake-up and the SNP's role in it, became paranoid about SNP involvement. Rather, voters on both sides of the border were overwhelmingly of the view that a hung parliament gave the SNP at least a chance of office. In Scotland, this was a position that the party could and did exploit.

FIGURE 1.2: PROPORTIONS OF SCOTTISH AND ENGLISH VOTERS GIVING SNP 'REAL CHANCE OF BEING PART OF THE NEXT UK GOVERNMENT'

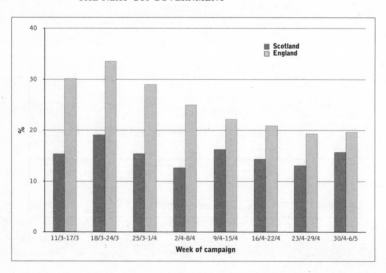

Naturally, the chances of the SNP being part of the government depended not only on a hung parliament but also on
the size of its parliamentary cohort. Recall that the third
condition for SNP success at Westminster elections is its viability and relevance running up to polling day. And here the
picture was equally clear-cut. Within around a month of the
referendum, the SNP had opened up a large lead in general
election polling and, as shown in Figure 1.3, the trend in the
vote intention poll of polls, that lead slowly but quite steadily increased as election day approached. That consistent
upward trend matches our argument about viability. The
more relevant the SNP appears likely to be in a Westminster
election, the more additional support it goes on to attract.

FIGURE 1.3: VOTE INTENTION 2015 POLL OF POLLS
        OCTOBER 2014–MAY 2015

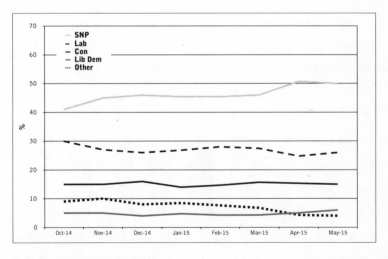

Source: What Scotland Thinks (2015)

The relevance criterion is a demanding one given that Scotland returns only fifty-nine MPs – under 10 per cent of the total – to Westminster. A Scottish-only party has to be very relevant indeed at home in order to be a significant player at Westminster. What was clear from the polls by the turn of the year was that the SNP had met this demand. We mentioned earlier that the electoral system creates tipping points; by going beyond the 40 per cent mark, the party had reached the point at which landslides were possible. So each new Scotland-wide poll was accompanied by vivid yellow maps illustrating the near-monopoly of seats implied by the SNP's vote share. And Lord Ashcroft's polls of individual constituencies provided no solace for any of the Unionist parties. Even when prompted with the names of prominent Labour and Liberal Democrat incumbents, which usually boosts support for said incumbents, most respondents still maintained that they would vote for the SNP candidates. While it was perhaps still hard to believe that the SNP would win the fifty-something seats projected from the polls, by early 2015 it was plain that the party was going to achieve major gains and send an unprecedentedly large cohort of MPs to Westminster.

These yellowed-out maps would have seemed less plausible had it not been for the 2011 Scottish Parliament result. In that election, the SNP had achieved something of a landslide in the constituency contests, winning fifty-three of seventy-three seats. While this success was not quite on the scale projected by the 2015 polls, it showed the party was capable of huge gains across the country and of winning erstwhile Labour fortresses in the west of Scotland. Politicians are fond of referring to elections as 'the only polls that matter'. In that respect, the SNP's claim to viability in 2015 was reinforced by its majority victory four years earlier.

In other respects, however, 2010 might have seemed the more relevant precedent. For exactly this reason of viability, the SNP has routinely performed better in Scottish than in UK general elections. And 2010 had seen Labour overturn a defeat at the preceding Holyrood election to become clearly Scotland's largest party with 42 per cent of the vote and forty-one of the fifty-nine seats. Scottish Labour's aim in 2015 was to recreate the conditions of 2010 as far as possible: to focus voters' minds on a straight Westminster fight between the Conservatives and Labour, and to warn – via the familiar theme of 'vote SNP, get Tory' – of the dangers of losing focus on that fight. The reasons why that failed, and more broadly why the 2015 general election in Scotland ended up looking nothing like 2010, only serve to underline our three conditions for SNP success.

First, the 2010 election was dominated by economic and fiscal crises, and arguments about which policy levers the UK government could and should pull to try to alleviate it. The Scottish dimension faded rather into the background. Insofar as it was significant, the prominence of Gordon Brown, Labour leader and a Scottish MP, helped Labour to assume the mantle of the Scottish party at Westminster. Brown had become an electoral liability in England but his popularity ratings in Scotland were appreciably higher. In stark contrast, the backdrop to 2015 was the referendum and ensuing arguments about further devolution. That meant an election fought on SNP rather than Labour territory. Second, although the polls anticipated a hung parliament, the Conservatives looked set throughout the campaign to be the largest party and a majority hardly looked out of the question. So a 'stop the Tories' message had more traction in Scotland in 2010 than it did in 2015, when the polls showed England and Wales as poised to prevent a Conservative majority without Scottish help. Also crucial here was Nicola Sturgeon's 2015 insistence on ruling out any support for a Conservative-led government. In this context, Scottish voters inclined to choose the SNP over Labour felt free to do so. Third, while the SNP had edged out Labour in the 2007 Holyrood contest, the party in 2010 was yet to be a convincing winner in any Scottish election and had spent virtually all of the 2005–10 parliament trailing Labour in the Westminster vote intention polls. Viability and relevance in a Westminster context would need to wait for a majority at Holyrood and then an extraordinary referendum and its aftermath.

A ONE-OFF STORM OR CLIMATE CHANGE?

In specifying these three conditions for SNP success at Westminster, we have so far avoided the question of what

might be called the logical relations between them. Specifically, are all three necessary for that success, or can the
presence of one compensate for the absence of another?
This apparently abstract question has immediate practical
relevance when we consider the long-term implications of
the 2015 outcome. Suppose (as many commentators do)
that in 2020 a Jeremy Corbyn-led Labour Party faces heavy
defeat across Britain and there is no glimpse of a hung parliament. Will the 'wasted vote' argument return and leave the
SNP struggling to maintain its vote share – and, in turn, its
viability next time around? Or does the scale of the party's
2015 landslide, and what looks set to be its continuing presence in office at Holyrood, mean that the SNP has made a
more enduring breakthrough?

The answer depends on several things, of which we highlight two here. One is the extent to which the current SNP
cohort in Westminster can be seen to make much of a difference. As we show in Chapter 5, voters are largely convinced
of the party's *commitment* to working in Scotland's interests,
but whether SNP members are seen as having the *capacity* to do so at Westminster is a different matter. The party's
efforts to style itself as the 'real opposition' to the Tories is
designed to counter future accusations of irrelevance should
the electoral arithmetic change. After all, if its MPs can make
a significant contribution in opposition to a majority government, a hung parliament ceases to be a necessary condition
for SNP relevance.

The second issue is the state of the party's chief rivals. Labour plays a prominent supporting role in this book given that its fall in Scotland and the SNP's rise are closely interlinked. At Westminster, the SNP's claims to be the 'real opposition' depend on whether that position is left vacant by a Labour Party that is too preoccupied by its own internal divisions and disappointing poll ratings. But at Holyrood, too, the SNP's long-term prospects depend on its battle with Labour for the centre-left vote. Some might see a major realignment in progress whereby the SNP is simply replacing Labour as Scotland's centre-left or, in the party's preferred term, 'progressive' party. This was the path charted for his party by Stephen Maxwell (1981) in an article that seemed far-fetched at the time of writing but now looks relevant. Others, however, might see the SNP's current dominance as a function of the constitutional flux that has made the 'Scottish interests' dimension – where it holds an apparently unassailable advantage – more relevant than the battle for office at Westminster, where Labour might remain Scotland's preferred option.

To that extent, our first condition – that the electoral context alerts voters to the perceived advantages of self-government – does look like a necessary precursor to continuing SNP success at Westminster. As we see in subsequent chapters, the SNP can win and has won Scottish Parliament elections based on 'domestic politics' – perceived advantages in governing competence, leadership and so on

– and even to some extent on downplaying the constitutional dimension. But the in-built disadvantage for the SNP in UK general elections – indeed, for any sub-state party at a state-wide election – means that their governing credentials are much less relevant. So the SNP may lose out when voters are concerned more with who governs at Westminster than with how far Scotland can gain autonomy from that government. A period of constitutional calm might therefore cause fifty-six to fall to somewhere nearer six. At the moment, however, such a period seems unlikely. It may be that the party's new-found strength at Westminster will survive everything except the fulfilment of its constitutional ambitions.

CHAPTER 2

'I'M NOT A NATIONALIST BUT...'

I n January 2014, Alex Salmond told interviewer Jim Naughtie that he regarded himself as British and that this was just part of his 'multi-layered' identity (Gardham, 2014). Scotland's then First Minister maintained that the referendum on independence was not about identity and quoted William McIlvanney, the Scottish novelist, who had described Scotland as a 'mongrel nation'. He insisted that Scots welcomed immigrants and were enthusiastic supporters of European Union membership. These comments were the sort that one might have expected from a European social democrat. (Indeed, if anything, by this point Salmond sounded much more enthusiastic about immigration than most social democrats.) But a nationalist? In fact, those who had followed SNP politics would not be at all surprised by these views. In this chapter we explore the SNP's nationalism, its perception of Scottish, British and other identities, how mainstream Salmond's views are within the wider party, and how Scottish identity and associated rhetoric feeds into the SNP's electoral strategy.

WHAT'S IN A NAME?

The names that political parties adopt are important. They signal the party's core support and objectives, and are central to how a party brands itself. A party may change its name when it has suffered a devastating defeat and the brand has become toxic or the name has lost resonance. In 1965, the Scottish Unionist Party changed its name to the Scottish Conservative and Unionist Party in order to be more closely aligned with the Conservative Party in the rest of Britain. The Unionist in the party's title was thought to have lost much of its meaning with the decline in importance of the union with Ireland which had originally inspired the name. In recent years, the Scottish Tories have debated another radical rebranding and a name change. Murdo Fraser, former deputy party leader in Scotland, proposed that the Conservative

Party should be wound up and a new party with a new name should be established in order to appeal to centre-right voters. He fought a leadership contest on this platform in 2011, winning the support of 45 per cent of party members in the run-off against Ruth Davidson (Convery, 2014). Less dramatically, the *New* Labour prefix was added as a way of distancing the party from its recent past.

The Scottish National Party was the name adopted when two parties merged in 1934 (Finlay, 1994). The National Party of Scotland (NPS), the larger party, was established in 1928 and grew out of disillusionment with the Labour Party in Scotland. Labour's failure to deliver Scottish home rule led some members to defect to create the new party. Its membership was tiny and drew predominantly from left-wing radicals. The Scottish (Self-Government) Party was set up in 1932. It styled itself the 'Moderates' to distinguish it from the NPS. Its membership included a few minor figures in the Scottish establishment: the Duke of Montrose; the Provost of Inverness; and Andrew Dewar Gibb, Regius Professor of Law at Glasgow University. Since neither party made any progress, however, they agreed to merge. Among its early leaders were R. B. Cunninghame Graham and Andrew Dewar Gibb. Almost half a century before, Cunninghame Graham had helped found the Scottish Labour Party with Keir Hardie and was elected to Parliament in 1886 on a platform that included abolishing the House of Lords; universal suffrage; nationalisation of land and mines; free school meals;

and an eight-hour working day. He was the first MP elected
to Parliament who declared himself to be a socialist (Bryant,
2015, p. 199). During his brief period in Parliament he was
suspended from the Commons three times – once for saying
'damn' in the Chamber – and was imprisoned while still an
MP for taking part in the 'Bloody Sunday' demonstration
at Trafalgar Square (Hansard, 9 February 1888, vol. 322,
col. 57). Dewar Gibb had a very different background. Having
been Winston Churchill's adjutant during the First World
War, he stood as a Unionist candidate in 1924 and 1929 and
saw Irish Catholic immigration as a threat to Scottish identity (Dewar Gibb, 1930). This radical/establishment tension
would run throughout the party's history and perplex opponents who struggled to understand this broad church.

The Scottish National Party was an uncontroversial name
when the party was formed in 1934. Far more important was
agreement on its objectives. The party's principal aim would be
'self-government', a sufficiently ambiguous term that allowed
for different views on relations with the rest of the United
Kingdom. Back then, the SNP's members included some who
were keen on what today would be referred to as 'devo-max',
including retaining a strong link with the British Empire.

Similarly, changing the party's name did not feature in
debates on how it might advance its cause as it languished on
the fringe of politics over the next three decades. SNP members believed that latent support for self-government was
suppressed by the strength of the electorate's identification

with established parties. The British Election Study of 1964 confirms that, in Scotland as in the rest of Britain, more than four out of five electors described themselves as 'very strong' or 'fairly strong' supporters of one of the three main Westminster parties. The party's fringe status meant that it rarely attracted criticism or attacks from Labour or the Scottish Unionists. That changed when the SNP started to pick up support in the mid-1960s, but the party was unlikely to see merit in changing its name just when it finally had become noticed.

There has always been ambiguity in how the party styles itself. Many senior members, including some of its leaders, have stressed that the party is called the Scottish *National* Party, suggesting a party that seeks to unite Scotland, rather than the Scottish *Nationalist* Party with all its negative connotations. Equally, some of the party's opponents have insisted on referring to the Scottish *Nationalist* Party, attempting to exploit nationalism's negative connotations. Yet, while objecting to 'nationalist' when it refers to the party, many within the SNP commonly use the term to describe its members and supporters. (When writing a book like this and seeking an alternative to endless repetition of 'the SNP', the synonym that comes most immediately to mind is 'the Nationalists'.) So this is not just a matter of slurs from the opposition: 'nationalists' as shorthand for SNP politicians, activists and supporters has become standard usage in Scottish politics.

This might sound like mere semantics and, even if it is probably more politically significant than that, it would be an exaggeration to suggest that the party's name has been a major problem for the SNP. Nonetheless, it has caused irritation when opponents have attempted to link the SNP's brand of 'civic' nationalism with those more 'ethnic' strands that blur into chauvinism, jingoism and racism. This sensitivity fuelled a determination to emphasise the party's civic side and, in particular, prompted some suggestions of a name change. In 1979, in common with other parties that have gone through a major defeat, especially after having high hopes shattered, the SNP looked inward. Douglas Crawford, MP for Perth and East Perthshire from 1974 to 1979, made just such a suggestion, but won little support and dropped the idea. Alex Salmond, then a young activist, considered proposing that the party should be renamed the Scottish Independence Party but also decided not to pursue the matter, accepting that there were dangers in losing a known brand. Instead, what the SNP sought to do from the 1980s onwards was to clarify the meaning of its nationalism. Rather than attempting a name change, then, the party – particularly under Alex Salmond's leadership – engaged in a conscious effort to define its version of nationalism in various ways that would make it difficult to associate it with ethnic nationalism. These are described over the course of this chapter.

Meanwhile, the question of names and labels remains potentially sensitive, as evidenced by examples of senior

members who decline to call themselves nationalist. On joining the SNP, Tommy Sheppard, now SNP MP for Edinburgh
East, declared, 'I'm not a nationalist, I remain a social
democrat, but my belief in social democracy will now be
advanced far better in the SNP' (*Edinburgh Evening News*,
25 September 2014). Sheppard was one of the SNP's new
recruits following the independence referendum. He was
a former deputy general secretary of the Scottish Labour
Party and came to the SNP with a suspicion of nationalism
but equally an awareness that it comes in various forms.
Nonetheless, it is doubtful whether, at earlier stages in the
party's history, a member who denied being a nationalist
would have been chosen to contest an election for the SNP.

The distinction between ethnic and civic nationalisms
is not only useful for analysing and comparing parties but
has also been used for rhetorical purposes in SNP politics.
In truth, both are forms of nationalism. The idea of the
nation lies at the core of nationalist ideology. The nation
was famously defined by the late Benedict Anderson as an
'imagined community', an association of people including
those who have never met nor could have ever met, having lived generations apart. One of the founding myths of
all nations is the idea of some historic roots. The appeal to
past glories or defeats is a feature of nations. SNP politicians have varied in their use of historical allusions. Nicola
Sturgeon rarely cites anything before the 1980s, when she
became politically aware, whereas Alex Salmond, holder of a

degree in medieval history, has often referred to Scotland as 'an ancient nation', as in the opening words to the preface to the independence White Paper published in September 2013 (Scottish Government, 2013, p. viii). Margaret Thatcher and William Wallace might seem unlikely allies but in different ways they helped forge modern Scottish nationalism.

For nationalists, the past is the same country. But that is true of civic as well as ethnic nationalisms and in other ideologies. Historical allusions are to be found across the range of political movements. Reference to the independent Scotland that existed before 1707 may have little practical relevance today but enhances the sense of Scotland as a distinct community. The danger for the SNP, and one the party has been aware of, is that emphasising the past creates a reactionary impression, a desire to return to a distant past. In the 1970s, Labour politicians would taunt the SNP by pointing out that Andrew Fletcher of Saltoun, who fought against the Act of Union of 1707, and after whom a nationalist think tank had been named, had been a supporter of slavery. So too had been many supporters of Union, of course. But it was the SNP members who had established a society invoking Fletcher's name.

THE SNP AND RELIGION

In common with the rest of Europe in the early to mid-twentieth century, the sense of national identity and nationalism was broadly ethnic. In the Scottish context that had less to do with race than religion. The anti-Catholicism within Scottish nationalism was part of a strand of prejudice found across Scottish society, including among staunch supporters of the Union. Even the Labour Party was not immune despite becoming the party to which Catholic voters gave overwhelming support. Religion was a significant cleavage in Scottish society and politics throughout the twentieth century (Budge and Urwin, 1966; Bennie et al., 1997). As late as 1987, Labour won almost three-quarters of the Catholic vote. The Labour Party in Scotland was unusual in Europe in being a left-of-centre party that won the bulk of Catholic voters. It did so more as the party of the underdog, representing a poor immigrant community, than on a confessional basis. Scottish Catholics had experienced discrimination and sections of the community felt insecure earlier in the century. The decline of the Conservatives in the Thatcher years left that party looking even more like a Protestant party as it fell back on its core support (Seawright and Curtice, 1995). The challenge for the SNP had long been the classic third-party challenge of breaking through a deeply entrenched religious cleavage. Just as the Liberals had found it easier to appeal to people with weak or no class identity, the SNP found it easier to win support among those with weak or no religious identity.

In the 1970s, the SNP approached the religious cleavage as it had the class cleavage in Scottish politics. It emphasised that it was a national party, attempting to appeal across social and other divisions. Yet the party struggled to make inroads into the west of Scotland working-class Catholic vote. When the SNP made its major breakthrough in 1974, it did so with relatively little support from those communities (Brand, 1978, p. 152). Scotland's sectarian divisions were holding the SNP back in the 1970s and 1980s.

It didn't help that the party included its own anti-Catholic element. Even if most within the party were aware of this strain, it nonetheless came as a shock when Billy Wolfe, former party leader and then holding the honorary position of party president, wrote a letter to the Church of Scotland's magazine opposing the first Papal visit to Scotland and the upgrading of the Vatican's representation to the UK in 1982. He later wrote a letter to *The Scotsman* expressing concerns that the Falklands would be taken over by a 'cruel and ruthless Fascist dictatorship of a Roman Catholic State' (Wilson, 2009, p. 211). This caused the SNP embarrassment and sparked accusations that the party was anti-Catholic. The party leadership condemned Wolfe's intervention. Gordon Wilson, SNP leader, denounced his 'bigoted anti-Catholic views' and asked him to resign as president. Wolfe refused to do so but decided against contesting the post that year.

Wilson also apologised to Cardinal Gordon Gray, the head of the Catholic Church in Scotland. It was testimony to the increasingly secure position of Catholics within Scottish society that Gray viewed the incident as causing discomfort for Catholic SNP members and sympathisers rather than as threatening the Catholic community as a whole. According to Tom Devine, eminent Scottish historian and leading figure in the Scottish Catholic community, by the 1990s Catholics aged under fifty-five had 'occupational parity' with fellow Scots and occupied the 'highest positions in government, universities, cultural institutions and the judiciary' (Devine, 2013). A mixture of public policy and religious leadership had brought about a transformation in the position of the Catholic community that worked to the SNP's advantage. State support for Catholic education provided a route into the middle class for many poorer Catholics, and the Labour Party was a powerful advocate for the community. The SNP only latterly tried to associate itself with these changes. While the process of appealing directly to Scottish Catholics had begun in the late 1980s, only in the 1990s did the party provide a coherent and coordinated strategy both for addressing claims of anti-Catholicism and, in turn, for making electoral inroads into this community.

In 1994, the Pope appointed a new Cardinal in Scotland. Cardinal Tom Winning was very sympathetic to the SNP. In a speech in Brussels in 1998, entitled 'A New Scotland in the New Europe', Winning described Scottish nationalism as 'mature, respectful of democracy and international in outlook' and argued that the 'sense of nationality and sense of European-ness which is emerging in Scotland' had little echo in the Europhobic British press. Scottish nationalism,

he maintained, had 'nothing in common with the aggressive and violent nationalism which has scarred the Balkans,
nor does it mirror the loud-mouthed rhetoric of the *Lega
Nord* in Italy or the xenophobic propaganda of the *Front
National* in France' (*The Herald*, 5 October 1998).

During Alex Salmond's first period as leader, the SNP
embarked on a series of initiatives designed to make
it easier for Catholics to vote for the party. The SNP was
emphatic in its support for the 1918 Education Act, which
enshrined state financial support for Catholic schools in
law. It had been opposed over the years not only by liberals who favoured the strict separation of Church and
state but also by anti-Catholic bigots. Labour and the
Conservatives had accepted the settlement, though mainly
without enthusiasm; the SNP went a step further and
embraced it on pluralistic grounds. Over the years, the
SNP would embrace a form of multiculturalism that placed
the 1918 education settlement at its heart. In his Cardinal
Winning Lecture in 2008, Alex Salmond argued that Catholic
schools should not be grudgingly accepted but celebrated
(Salmond, 2008).

Pockets of sectarianism still existed, a notorious example
being Monklands in North Lanarkshire. The local council
was riven with sectarian divisions over accusations that predominantly Catholic Coatbridge was favoured in levels of
spending over predominantly Protestant Airdrie by the ruling Labour council that was itself almost entirely Catholic

in make-up. These tensions came to a head in 1994 during the Monklands East by-election following the death of John Smith, the Labour Party leader and local MP. Neither Kay Ullrich, the SNP candidate, nor Labour's Helen Liddell was keen to engage with the issue but it proved difficult to avoid. Embarrassed at the UK media spotlight on the unsavoury nature of local politics in a constituency represented by its late leader, Labour attempted to redirect attention onto its opponents, the eventual winner Liddell in her victory speech accusing the SNP of 'playing the Orange card'. It proved a salutary experience for the SNP which increased its efforts to engage directly with the Catholic community, and publicly disowned any suggestion that the last vestiges of sectarianism could be left to die away on their own.

The party established a group under Mike Russell, then SNP chief executive, to consider how best to advance its cause among Catholics. This group included some prominent Catholic party members. The main outcome of these meetings was to urge the leadership to campaign against the Act of Settlement's provisions preventing a Catholic from becoming monarch (Scottish Parliamentary Corporate Body, 1999). This was a difficult area for the SNP as it wanted to avoid causing offence to the monarchy while also assuaging its large republican element. In 1977, during the Queen's Silver Jubilee celebrations, the party had suffered when the Queen had declared that she could not forget that she was 'crowned Queen of the United Kingdom of Great Britain and Northern Ireland'. Many within the SNP concluded that the monarchy would always be used to undermine the SNP and that the party should meet this challenge head on, while others saw little advantage in adding republicanism to the party's baggage. Ultimately, the party's attitude has been similar to Labour's in preferring to avoid the tricky subject altogether. In this case, however, the leadership calculated that carefully articulated opposition to the Act of Settlement might meet its goal of showing support to the Catholic community without causing too much offence to the Queen. This was a classic example of symbolic politics, with no practical implications for the voters that the SNP hoped to attract.

Mike Russell would continue campaigning on this issue following his election as an MSP in 1999. In December of that year, he moved a resolution in the Scottish Parliament on the Act of Settlement (Scottish Parliament, 14 December 1999). This again was purely symbolic, given that such matters were retained by Westminster under devolution. However, these gestures contributed to the SNP's image as a party sympathetic to the Catholic community, and began to undermine Labour's pre-eminent position as representative of the Catholic community in Scotland.

In recent years, any efforts to suggest that the SNP still harboured anti-Catholic sentiment became confined to the fringe of politics. During the independence referendum, George Galloway, former Labour and Respect MP, sought to play the Catholic card, insisting that there was a 'historic crossover between Scottish nationalism and anti-Irish Roman Catholicism' (*Sunday Herald*, 19 May 2013). But what might have been effective in Galloway's days as a young Labour organiser in Dundee no longer worked. Insofar as those who sought them could find examples of anti-Catholic sentiment in the SNP, this made it no different from any other large organisation in Scotland – few were likely to be convinced that such views were mainstream. In 2014, 58 per cent of Scottish Catholics voted for independence and 42 per cent for the Union – almost the reverse of the situation among Scotland's Protestant community. Catholics thus showed even stronger support for independence than the slight majority 'Yes' vote among those who had no religious affiliation, the group that had shown most support for the SNP when it first appeared as a serious force in Scottish politics forty years before. And, as we show in Chapter 8, Catholics are increasingly strongly represented among the SNP vote in both Holyrood and Westminster elections – again, a major change from just a few decades ago.

NEW AND ASIAN SCOTS

This religious positioning was only part of a wider strategy to emphasise the SNP's liberal multiculturalism. In two other important respects, the SNP set out to overcome accusations that it harboured illiberal tendencies. The first was to challenge notions that the SNP was anti-English. The second was to affirm its positive attitude regarding recent immigration. The two overlap, given that the English in Scotland have been described as 'by far Scotland's largest minority grouping' (McIntosh et al., 2004), with the 2011 census confirming that 9 per cent of those living in Scotland at the time had been born in England. But of course the nature and origins of opposition to English immigration are different from those concerning immigration from elsewhere, giving the SNP two rhetorical fronts on which to assert its openness and civic approach to nationality and identity.

All identities are defined to some extent in contradistinction to some *other*, but that other may be fluid. The 'other' in SNP politics, as in Scottish society, has never been quite so simple as England or the English. Scottish nationalism's other has been remarkably flexible, taking on a variety of forms among which the most prevalent is Unionism, essentially a form of British or UK nationalism. Nonetheless, while there is a strain of anti-English sentiment in Scottish society well beyond the SNP, it is not hard to see why the party would, from its establishment, have faced particular accusations of anti-Englishness.

For one thing, it had members like Hugh MacDiarmid, Scottish poet and leading figure in the literary renaissance (and also a member of the Communist Party), who would list Anglophobia among his hobbies in *Who's Who*. In its

early period, the party was less well known than such colourful figures who, even if on the margins of the nationalist
movement, attracted more media attention than did the sober
SNP leadership. Another example is Wendy Wood, whose
rhetoric left little doubt about her views of England and the
English and whose civil disobedience in campaigning for
Scottish independence led at one stage to her being imprisoned. While the party had always had English members too,
including prominent figures, it only took one fringe figure
making some anti-English comment to cause the leadership
a headache. Robert McIntyre, who was the SNP's first ever
MP, elected briefly in a by-election just before the 1945 general election, and a leading figure in the SNP through to the
1980s, would complain bitterly about Wood's antics and
maintain that she did more harm than good.

In 1967, a group calling itself the 1320 Club was set up,
named in recognition of the Declaration of Arbroath of that
year, and including a few of the more flamboyant characters,
including MacDiarmid and Wood. When it drew up plans
for a provisional Scottish government, including an army
to combat some imagined English attack, it was proscribed
by the SNP. The 1320 Club was eventually disbanded but
Sìol nan Gàidheal (SNG), gaelic for Seed of the Gael, took
its place in the late 1970s. SNG was a reaction to the SNP's
support for devolution at that time, which had led some to
conclude that the SNP was not a true nationalist party. While
remaining on the periphery of Scottish nationalism, it came

to attention after the SNP suffered heavy defeats in 1979 and activists sought easy solutions to advance. SNG was the SNP's Militant Tendency – though SNG members dressed in militaristic uniform – and it was banned by the SNP at its 1982 annual conference. SNG has subsequently been revived twice but successively moving further into the fringe. The 1980s and 1990s also saw the emergence of anti-English groups such as 'Scottish Watch' and 'Settler Watch', which claimed to keep a record of English people given prominent positions in Scotland. These groupuscules generated more media attention than they merited given their size and relevance. While a much earlier Scottish Watch had been set up by Wendy Wood to oppose an English takeover of Scotland, these later versions took inspiration more from direct-action elements in Welsh nationalism – although they never engaged in anything approaching the burning of holiday homes – and their interactions with the mainstream SNP were largely confined to having their membership revoked.

There was a Walter Mitty element to some of those involved in these fringe organisations. As Alex Salmond has often remarked, there has never been so much as a nosebleed in the name of Scottish nationalism. The SNP was quick to expel anyone known to be associated with these groups. Efforts by its opponents to link the SNP to such elements might have been more successful in the past when the party was relatively unknown. But, as the SNP became more successful, its image would be formed by its leaders rather than the fringe.

The distance between the two was inadvertently exposed by a 2010 sub-headline in the *Daily Express*: 'An oil industry contractor who has shaken hands with Alex Salmond has claimed to be the founder of racist organisation Settler Watch' (Mills, 2010).

The SNP continues to combat an image problem on the fringe of the national movement. Social media is now the medium of choice for anti-social comments in general and anti-English comments in particular. When these are posted or tweeted by those also proclaiming support for the SNP, this strain is inescapably associated with the party. Many of the comments that have led to expulsions from the party have tended to be personally offensive – such as those attacking J. K. Rowling – rather than specifically Anglophobic in content. (There is also plenty of vitriol poured on those Scots who oppose independence and have been condemned as 'Quislings' – or worse – as a result.) Yet Anglophobia runs through Scottish society and is far from confined to the SNP and its supporters. The same goes for Twitter trolling, as gruesomely shown when tennis player Andy Murray announced his support for independence and faced references to the mass shooting in Dunblane that he narrowly escaped.

More broadly, judging or labelling a party by its supporters' private utterances is a harsh test that most or all would fail. The SNP is not in the same position as UKIP, which has often felt obliged to censure its own elected officials and candidates for various forms of political incorrectness gone mad.

While a colourful intake of SNP MPs following the general election meant a stream of old social media posts through which journalists or opponents could search, the most they could dredge up by way of anti-Englishness was Mhairi Black's teenage gloating over England's footballing failure at the 2010 World Cup. If the SNP should be judged instead by its own rhetoric, Iain Macwhirter sounds right when asserting that 'any trace of ethnic nationalism, and anti-English sentiment, was expunged from the party in the 1970s' (*The Herald*, 18 June 2015). If it should be judged by how strongly and consistently it clamps down on those members who do cross the line, again the party largely lives up to Macwhirter's claim. Perhaps the most vivid illustration of the SNP leadership's determined avoidance of Anglophobia came when exit polls in 2014 revealed that independence had been rejected by a decisive majority of English-born voters but narrowly supported by those born in Scotland. The party's nationalism stayed resolutely civic, with nothing made of the difference. The comparison with the 1995 Quebec referendum is instructive. Following his side's narrow defeat, Jacques Parizeau, leader of the Parti Québécois, asserted that French speakers had voted for sovereignty-association and blamed the outcome on 'l'argent et le vote ethnique'.

Scotland has never had a large ethnic minority population despite its strong links with the Empire and Commonwealth (see Table 2.1). By far the largest of the small minorities – that is, after English-born people living in Scotland – is

TABLE 2.1: ETHNIC PROFILE OF SCOTTISH POPULATION,
            2011 CENSUS

	% OF TOTAL POPULATION	% OF MINORITY ETHNIC POPULATION (ROUNDED ESTIMATE)	BASE
African	0.6	14	30,000
Asian / Asian Scottish / Asian British	2.7	67	141,000
Caribbean or Black	0.1	3	7,000
Mixed / multiple ethnic group	0.4	9	20,000
Other ethnic group	0.3	7	14,000
White	96.0	n/a	5,084,000
All minority ethnic population	4.0	100	211,000
TOTAL POPULATION	**100**	**n/a**	**5,295,000**

Source: The Scottish Government Summary: Ethnic Group Demographics
http://www.gov.scot/Topics/People/Equality/Equalities/DataGrid/Ethnicity/EthPopMig

Scotland's Asian, largely Pakistani, community. Historically, in Scotland as in the rest of Britain, this community has tended to give strong support to the Labour Party. However, as with Catholics, the SNP made a concerted effort to win over Asian voters. Given the small numbers involved, this was less about direct electoral gain and more about symbolism. The party was keen to demonstrate that it had support among Scotland's ethnic minority community in order to emphasise its civic nationalism. In 1995, the Asian Scots for Independence group was set up with strong support from the SNP leadership. Its founding member was Bashir Ahmad, brought up in Pakistan before moving to Scotland when he was twenty-one. He became the first Asian MSP when elected on the SNP's Glasgow list in 2007.

While the SNP had for some time made strenuous efforts to attract support among Scotland's Asian community, it was the war in Iraq that allowed the party to start reaping the benefits. Between 2001 and 2003, a large part of Scotland's Muslim community shifted its allegiance from Labour to SNP (Hussain and Miller, 2006). The ground had been well prepared but it was disillusionment with Labour that seems to have proved decisive. The somewhat non-committal language is necessary here because, given the small ethnic minority population in Scotland, the typical opinion poll provides insufficient numbers to estimate Asians' voting patterns. (The Ethnic Minority British Election Survey included only thirty-nine Scots.) Nonetheless, as we show in Chapter 8, there are grounds to conclude that there has indeed been a significant swing from Labour to the SNP among Scottish Asians.

While acknowledging the leadership's resolutely civic perspective, sceptics might wonder whether the SNP's grass-roots are equally convinced that immigrants from England, Pakistan or anywhere else can be just as Scottish as those born and raised in the country. And the party has not been immune from racism rows in local politics (e.g. *Daily Record*, 8 February 2016) but is in this respect no different from any other party. One way of testing this commitment at the grassroots is via a 2007 survey, in which party members were asked about how important were various characteristics for a person to be considered 'truly Scottish'. Table 2.2 suggests two things about the members' views. First, there is a widespread acceptance of the leadership's civic conception of national identity. Hardly any respondents dismissed 'feeling Scottish' and 'respecting Scottish political institutions', the hallmarks of voluntary membership of a political community, as unimportant. And living in Scotland was seen as more important than having been born in Scotland.

TABLE 2.2: IMPORTANCE OF CHARACTERISTICS FOR BEING 'TRULY SCOTTISH'

HOW IMPORTANT IS ___ TO BE TRULY SCOTTISH?	VERY	FAIRLY	NOT VERY	NOT AT ALL
To have Scottish ancestry	24	32	27	17
To have been born in Scotland	33	30	22	15
To live in Scotland now	48	32	15	6
To have lived in Scotland for most of one's life	28	37	26	9
To be a Christian	12	13	19	56
To respect Scottish political institutions and laws	59	34	5	2
To feel Scottish	78	18	3	1
To be able to speak English, Gaelic or Scots	39	34	17	10

Source: Mitchell et al., 2012, p. 110

Second, however, only a minority – albeit a large one – dismisses the two most obviously ethnic characteristics, having Scottish ancestry and being born in Scotland, as unimportant. Most regard ancestry and birth as aspects of Scottishness, while acknowledging other routes to the same destination. As David McCrone puts it, 'The first thing to be said is that in modern Scotland we live quite happily with multiple meanings of what it means to be a Scot: by birth, descent and residence' (2001, p. 156). It appears that this is also true of SNP members.

THE SNP AND BRITISHNESS

For all this commentary on civic and ethnic nationalism, at least as important here is the distinction between state nationalism and sub-state or minority nationalism, sometimes referred to respectively as 'official' and 'regional' national-ism (Keating, 1988; Kellas, 1998). Any state requires that its citizenry has some measure of identification with that state. Without this, the government's legitimacy is called into ques-tion and it is required to enforce its rule without consent. Scottish nationalists do not question the legitimacy of the UK state or government. The nearest to a UK legitimacy prob-lem arose in the 1980s and 1990s when the Conservatives, governing with declining support, were perceived to impose their will against the wishes of the Scots. In the rhetoric of the time, there was a 'democratic deficit' in Scotland. But that did not lead to anything more than a growth in the demand for a Scottish Parliament. SNP members were conscious that Labour, Scotland's largest party, opposed independence and any claim that the UK government lacked legitimacy was weakened by Labour's support for the Union.

The shrillest voices arguing that the Conservatives at that time had no legitimacy often came from within the Labour Party. In 1984, Labour's Scottish conference passed a resolution stating that the Conservative government had 'no mandate' in Scotland and after the 1989 election, a wing of the party proposed that its candidates should seek a 'dual mandate' so that in the event of a majority of Scottish Labour MPs being returned while the Conservatives won across the UK, its Scottish MPs would withdraw from the House of Commons to establish a Scottish Parliament (Mitchell, 1998). Labour's Scottish leadership succeeded in kicking this proposal into the long grass. The party's nationalism appeared to be straightforwardly instrumental: an element within the Labour Party was willing to be Scottish or British depending on the outcome of elections. The relationship between Scottish and British nationalisms is more complex than adversarial debates allow, and UK and Scottish nationalisms share more than their respective supporters would care to admit. Each is civic and constitutional. Given the SNP's majority victory in the Scottish election of 2011, the UK government conceded that a referendum on Scottish independence should be held. For its part, the Scottish government immediately accepted the result of the referendum. At no point has the SNP advocated Sinn Féin's tactics of parliamentary abstention, let alone its association with violence.

Each nationalism has its myths and historical allusions to draw upon. UK nationalists were keen in the run-up to the referendum to emphasise their state's common past, just as Scottish nationalists are keen to refer to the antiquity of the Scottish nation. If anything, this aspect of nationalism was even more evident in London's Olympics than in Glasgow's Commonwealth Games two years later. First, the Olympic torch weaved its way around the whole of the UK. Then Danny Boyle's opening ceremony was described by Tristram Hunt, Labour MP and historian, as a celebration of 'our shared icons of the National Health Service and monarchy, of film and music'. He added that 'conservatives should thank Boyle for the most gifted celebration of the Act of Union in a generation' (Hunt, 2012). Scottish nationalism's primary counterpoint is not socialism, liberalism or conservatism but British or UK nationalism, and its secondary counterpoint will be whichever ideology is in the ascendant in the UK state at that given moment.

The SNP traditionally won almost all of its support among that section of the population that described itself as 'Scottish, not British'. At its foundation and through its early years, its leadership feared that the very idea of Scotland was under threat through assimilation via the media and other facets of modernisation. This cultural nationalism was not always associated with support for the party or its objectives, but it informed the movement in its early stages. As late as the 1970s, senior SNP figures – notably Billy Wolfe – were concerned that Scottish identity was under threat. In this sense, identity politics had played a significant part in the party's foundation and early development.

However, a process of change began in the 1980s as identity was downgraded in SNP politics. While it has not disappeared, it has become less significant compared not only with the past but also with the politics of other nationalist parties elsewhere. In Quebec and Wales, for example, language and culture animate nationalist discourse in a way that is absent in Scotland. Bill 101 passed by the Parti Québécois in 1977, for instance, gave priority to the French language, including stipulating that all signs had to be in French. Welsh language activists engaged in radical activities including burning down English-owned holiday homes in defence of Welsh language and culture. There was no equivalent of either in Scotland. In large measure this was because the sense of a threat to Scottish identity disappeared. In 1990, George Kerevan, then a Labour councillor but now SNP MP for East Lothian, wrote that, while the 1979 devolution referendum had been a defeat, there had been an 'explosion of cultural activity in Scotland in the Seventies and Eighties' which amounted to 'a declaration of cultural independence' (Kerevan, 1990, p. 27). The perceived threat to

Scottish identity had been replaced by the perceived threat posed by Thatcherism to Scottish institutions and values. The argument was that the increasing divergence of Scottish and English voting behaviour reflected these distinctive Scottish values. So, as the SNP's 'other' mutated into Thatcherism, Scottish identity in turn became a more explicitly political identity for many Scots. As discussed above, Labour was also playing the Scottish card and ensuring that the SNP did not monopolise an emerging consensus among most Scottish voters. Indeed, for much of the 1980s, Labour would claim to be *the* Scottish party.

The triumph of politics over identity in Scottish nationalism can be illustrated by the 2007 SNP membership survey that we referred to earlier. The relevant question was: 'Over the years, there has been talk of many different potential threats to the Scottish nation. Which of these do you think *are* or *were* particularly important threats?' Members were asked to rank three from a list of threats (see Table 2.3). The first thing to say is that, consistent with earlier arguments, English nationalism and immigration from England were barely mentioned – and neither, for that matter, was immigration from anywhere else. By contrast, three of the four most cited threats are straightforwardly political and, while the perceived lack of self-confidence may have had a cultural component, by this point in time – with these SNP members looking with frustration at the flatlining poll support for independence – it probably also had major political and economic components

as well. It is striking that Thatcherism was still seen by quite
a few members, including those who had joined the party
long after her departure from the scene (Mitchell et al., 2011,
p. 94), as a major threat.

TABLE 2.3: PERCEIVED THREATS TO THE SCOTTISH NATION

THREATS	RANKED MOST IMPORTANT %	NOT RANKED AT ALL %
Being denied North Sea oil revenues	24	41
Lack of self-confidence as a nation	23	55
London government	17	51
Thatcherism	11	75
Nuclear weapons	6	75
Foreign ownership of Scottish businesses	3	84
Nuclear waste	3	86
Mass media	2	86
Emigration	2	89
European Union policies	2	91
Immigration from outside the UK	2	92
Immigration from England	2	93
English nationalism	1	97

Source: SNP membership survey, 2007

By the time devolution was established, then, the SNP's leadership was sufficiently relaxed about identity issues to be
willing to recognise the role of Britishness within Scotland,
even if few went as far as Alex Salmond in the remarks that
opened this chapter and embraced a British identity of their

own. Andrew Wilson, a young SNP MSP, delivered a lecture at the SNP's annual conference in 1999 suggesting that
Britishness would survive independence and wrote a newspa-
per column suggesting that Scots should support the English
football team in the 2002 World Cup. He asserted that the
real problem was the British political Union and not the social
Union (*The Economist*, 23 September 1999). This was not
the first occasion on which the idea that some form of British
institutional arrangement could exist after independence had
been floated within the SNP. At the height of its electoral fortunes in the 1970s, the SNP had proposed that there should
be a Council of the Isles and had referred to the social Union
that would continue to exist after independence. But the issue
slipped off the SNP's agenda during the 1980s, only to return
as the SNP advanced again.

At the time, Andrew Wilson's proposals were a step too
far for some of his fellow SNP members. There remained a
strong strand in the party that remained hostile to Britishness,
and Wilson's adventurous line was part of the reason why he
lost out in the battle for a place sufficiently high on the SNP
list in 2003 to secure re-election to the Scottish Parliament.
Yet his message on Britishness would soon become ortho-
doxy inside the party, especially his argument that the SNP
confronted a 'glass ceiling' in its appeal by concentrating on
those with a Scottish identity.

It is clear that that glass ceiling has not been broken yet.
This is highlighted in Table 2.4, which shows the relationship

TABLE 2.4: SNP VOTE BY NATIONAL IDENTITY;
NATIONAL IDENTITY BY SNP VOTE, 1992–2015

	1992	1997	2001	2005	2010	2015
% OF THESE IDENTIFIERS WHO VOTED SNP:						
Scottish not British	46	29	26	25	36	77
More Scottish than British	26	22	17	19	23	67
More or equally British	12	11	9	7	8	19
% OF SNP VOTERS WHO IDENTIFY AS:						
Scottish not British	36	35	51	46	48	56
More Scottish than British	44	45	31	40	37	29
More or equally British	20	20	17	15	15	15

Sources: SES, 1992, 1997; SSA, 2001, 2005, 2010; BES, 2015

between national identity and SNP voting over recent
decades. It is based on what has become a standard survey
question asking people whether they feel purely Scottish or
British, both equally, or both but with a leaning towards
one side. In the table, we combine all those who feel at least
equally British, partly because the numbers who feel mostly
or only British are quite small and also because the SNP polls
similarly (poorly) among each group. The upper half of the
table records the proportion of people with a given identity who voted SNP in that year's general election. Then the
lower half records the proportion of the SNP's vote coming

from each group – that is, the national identity profile of the party's support. The results for 'More or equally British' are highly consistent in each half of the table. Unsurprisingly, the SNP polls consistently poorly among those who feel at least as British as Scottish, and these voters consequently make up a relatively small proportion of its vote. Not until its 2015 landslide did the party show signs of electoral headway within that group, and even then its relative importance to the party did not change (with these voters still making up just 15 per cent of the SNP's support). Arguably, the SNP was no less a party for Scottish identifiers in 2015; it was just a much more successful such party.

Given the persistence of British identity and its influence over Scottish voting behaviour, the SNP's prospects of advancing required them to do at least one of two things: winning over more of those with a primarily but not exclusively Scottish identity, and making British identity less important in electoral behaviour. Much of this book is devoted to explaining how the SNP was able to win over so many of its potential supporters and thus achieve figures like the 77 per cent and 67 per cent in Table 2.4. For present purposes, there are two key points. The first is that the SNP's growing electoral appeal over the past decade or so was based in large part on aspects like governing competence and leadership that should have appeal across the national identity spectrum. This paid particular dividends in the 2011 Scottish Parliament election, in which the SNP won 24 per cent of the vote – two percentage points more than the Conservatives – among those reporting themselves 'British, not Scottish'. Second, the party ceased any attempts to 'convert' British identifiers or to imply that such an identity was incompatible with the SNP's political ambitions. The Union was portrayed as trampling not on Scottish identity per se but on Scottish political values, priorities and interests. The 'other' thus became a political position rather than an identity, and the SNP came to have a relaxed attitude towards Britishness.

CONCLUSION

In arguing that Britishness would survive Scottish independence, Alex Salmond was offering an opinion rather than making a policy statement. Nation-building can be sponsored by government, but ultimately identity is a personal and subjective matter. But by acknowledging Britishness while retaining an emphasis on Scottishness in the SNP's language, the SNP made it easier for those who retained at least some British identity – that is, the clear majority of Scots – to support the party. The culmination of this process was evident in that 2011 Scottish election, in which the SNP outpolled the Conservatives among the 'British not Scottish' voters. This might say as much about the weakness of the Scottish Conservatives but it also points to significant SNP headway well beyond its core vote. Not surprisingly, it proved a lot more difficult to downplay the role of Britishness in the context of an independence referendum, and one question for Chapter 7 is whether that campaign may have reversed some of the progress that the party of 'Yes' had made among British identifiers.

The referendum also provided an acid test of the SNP's self-professed civic nationalism when exit polls revealed that the Scottish-born electorate had actually voted narrowly in favour of independence. It was those who had come into Scotland who were sufficiently numerous and sceptical of independence to swing the vote the other way. Given SNP rhetoric over decades, it would have been a handbrake turn had it questioned the legitimacy of the outcome as a result. But the party's refusal to make anything of this point under-lines that this is not merely rhetoric but goes deeper.

We are left with the question of whether a party should be judged by its own rhetoric and policy or by the 140-character manifestos of some of its followers. Even if no party would want to face the latter test, this is an especially pertinent question for a party whose *raison d'être* is nation-alism, however civic its own brand. As Alex Massie puts it: 'The SNP really is different from many other nationalist par-ties even if, unavoidably, it also wins support from plenty of people who might easily, in other circumstances, find a home in those other kinds of nationalist parties' (*The Spectator*, 19 June 2015). In truth, it wins rather little of its *electoral* support from the people Massie describes, and even less if the allusion is to anti-immigrant nationalist parties such as in Belgium or France. That strand of opinion is much better catered for by other parties. In the absence of a more aggressively separatist force, the SNP may remain the party affiliation of choice for the vocal minority of Anglophobes on Twitter. However, the party's reputation for civic nationalism was earned partly by tirelessly distancing itself from such fringes.

CHAPTER 3

DEVOLUTION DIVIDEND

At the end of the previous chapter, we discussed the SNP's recent strategies for winning the votes of those with primarily British rather than Scottish identity. This is a measure of the party's new-found success. The SNP spent most of the period up to and including 1997 being comprehensively outpolled by Labour even among those with a primarily Scottish identity. In that sense the party was failing to win over the natural constituency of Scottish nationalism, let alone extend it. There are a number of reasons for this but three were clearly highlighted in Chapter 1 – they are simply the obverse of the conditions that we listed under which the SNP would enjoy success at Westminster elections. First, the Scottish dimension was often eclipsed in election campaigns focused on the battle for Downing Street. Second, the first-past-the-post system meant that one of those two parties was often set for a thumping majority, offering little scope for the SNP – or any other smaller force – to exert any influence. Third, at least until the 1970s and even to some extent during the 1980s, the SNP sometimes struggled to appear relevant even within Scottish politics. If significant numbers of voters who might have been inclined to support the SNP were not doing so, then fear of wasting their votes is likely to have been a key reason.

On all three counts, things looked different in elections to the Scottish Parliament. While Westminster politics would remain an important part of the backdrop for devolved elections, they were much less likely to crowd out Scottish concerns. The more proportional electoral system meant that all parties were potentially parties of government. According to polls, the SNP went into the first devolved election as the country's second-largest party. More broadly, the new political arena established with the Scottish Parliament created a range of new opportunities for the SNP. In this chapter, we set out the potential that devolution offered to the SNP, consider why it took time for that potential to be realised, and map the electoral battleground on which the party hoped to secure this devolution dividend.

OPPORTUNITIES

The primary reason why devolution offered new opportunities for the SNP is also the simplest. In the 1997 UK general election, the SNP won a healthy 22 per cent of the vote and 8 per cent of the seats in Scotland. But this amounted to just 2 per cent of the UK vote and 1 per cent – six out of 659 – of the seats in Westminster. A party standing in only one rather small part of the United Kingdom will inevitably be peripheral in general elections unless – as in 2015 – that party does extremely well in its own territory *and* has the chance via a hung parliament of influencing government formation. In this sense, Scottish-only devolved elections did not offer any particular advantage to the SNP; they just eliminated a huge disadvantage in terms of viability.

The mixed-member proportional system installed for devolved elections was also expected to be kinder to the SNP in two respects. (It would later turn out to be kind in a third, largely unforeseen, respect.) First, it offset the disadvantage that the party suffered under the first-past-the-post system due to the relatively even geographic spread of its vote. We just noted that the party won only 8 per cent of seats based on a 22 per cent vote share in Scotland in the 1997 election. Such a pattern probably sounds familiar to Liberal Democrats and so will the reason for it, because that party faced the same problem in England: winning a respectable vote share across large parts of the country but rarely enough to win first-past-the-post seats. By contrast, the Liberal Democrats in Scotland actually enjoyed the kind of concentrated vote that helps under such a system. In the first-past-the-post constituency contests at the first Holyrood election in 1999, the Liberal Democrats' vote share dipped under 5 per cent in three seats but reached 67 per cent in Orkney and was over or close to 50 per cent in other strongholds. By contrast, nowhere did the SNP vote share dip into single figures but only Alex Salmond in Banff and Buchan managed over 50 per cent.

To assess this more systematically, we calculated how much a party's vote share varied across Scotland's seventy-three constituencies at this first Scottish Parliament election. The exact values of these 'coefficients of variation' are not especially meaningful; what matters is the comparison: larger numbers mean a more uneven performance across the country. The Liberal Democrats' coefficient was comfortably the largest (0.87), reflecting its very strong showings in certain strongholds like Orkney and Shetland, while the SNP recorded the smallest (0.26), with Labour's (0.34) not far away. These small coefficients of variation mean that the SNP's showing rarely climbed far above the party's overall 29 per cent vote share while Labour's rarely dipped far below its nationwide 39 per cent. This is why Labour was able to win fifty-three constituency seats while the SNP took just seven – fewer than the Liberal Democrats despite winning more than double the Lib Dems' national vote share. (See Table 3.1 for a full breakdown of the results of all four Scottish Parliament elections to date.)

TABLE 3.1 RESULTS OF SCOTTISH PARLIAMENT ELECTIONS, 1999–2011

1999	CONSTITUENCIES		REGIONAL LIST		TOTAL	
	VOTES (%)	SEATS	VOTES (%)	SEATS	SEATS	SEATS (%)
Conservative	15.6	0	15.4	18	18	13.9
Labour	38.8	53	33.8	3	56	43.4
Lib Dem	14.2	12	12.5	5	17	13.2
SNP	28.7	7	27.5	28	35	27.1
Green			3.6	1	1	0.8
Others	2.7	1	7.2	1	2	1.6

2001	CONSTITUENCIES		REGIONAL LIST		TOTAL	
	VOTES (%)	SEATS	VOTES (%)	SEATS	SEATS	SEATS (%)
Conservative	16.6	3	15.5	15	18 (n.c.)	14.2
Labour	34.6	46	29.3	4	50 (-6)	39.4
Lib Dem	15.3	13	11.8	4	17 (n.c.)	13.4
SNP	23.8	9	20.9	18	27 (-8)	21.3
Green			6.9	7	7 (+6)	5.5
Others	9.7	2	15.8	8	8 (+6)	6.3

2007	CONSTITUENCIES		REGIONAL LIST		TOTAL	
	VOTES (%)	SEATS	VOTES (%)	SEATS	SEATS	SEATS (%)
Conservative	16.6	4	13.9	13	17 (-1)	13.2
Labour	32.2	37	29.2	9	46 (-4)	35.7
Lib Dem	16.2	11	11.3	5	16 (-1)	12.4
SNP	32.9	21	31.0	26	47 (+20)	36.4
Green	0.2	0	4.0	2	2 (-5)	1.6
Others	1.9	0	10.6	1	1 (-7)	0.8

2011	CONSTITUENCIES		REGIONAL LIST		TOTAL	
	VOTES (%)	SEATS	VOTES (%)	SEATS	SEATS	SEATS (%)
Conservative	13.9	3	12.4	12	15 (-2)	11.6
Labour	31.7	15	26.3	22	37 (-9)	28.7
Lib Dem	7.9	2	5.2	3	5 (-11)	3.9
SNP	45.4	53	44.0	16	69 (+22)	53.5
Green	-	-	4.4	2	2 (n.c.)	1.6
Others	1.1	0	7.7	1	1 (n.c.)	.8

But, of course, in Holyrood elections there were also regional list seats, designed to correct for exactly this kind of disproportionality. The SNP won exactly half of those list seats in 1999, making up four-fifths of its parliamentary representation. This heavy reliance on the lists came to have its disadvantages, notably that candidates' campaigning efforts are spent within their party on obtaining the kind of list position that more or less guarantees election, rather than on the ground campaigning against other parties for constituency seats. But the most striking feature of the party's first Holyrood cohort was its sheer size. While this was not surprising given the new electoral context, it did mean that more SNP parliamentarians were elected in 1999 than in all previous elections combined. Devolution thus also greatly extended the party's powers of patronage via candidate selection.

The proportional component in the system was not just about giving each party its fair share. It was also about avoiding single-party dominance. There was indeed a longer-term fear among Unionist parties that the SNP might gain a majority of seats and use that position to press strongly for independence. But the more realistic short-term prospect was of landslide Labour majorities based on a minority of votes. In the 1979 referendum, campaigners against devolution had made much of the prospect of a Labour monopoly on power. And the constituency results in 1999, with Labour taking 74 per cent of the seats based on 39 per cent of the vote, confirm that a Scottish Parliament elected under first-past-the-post would have made Scotland look more like a one-party state rather than the multi-party system – albeit with Labour as clearly the leading force – that it had been since the early 1980s. For the SNP at the time of devolution, then, proportional representation was not a frustrating concession denying it a potential majority. It was an essential condition for a pluralist Parliament in which they could play a meaningful part.

That Labour seemed unlikely to secure a Holyrood majority offered the SNP, as all parties in the Scottish Parliament, the opportunity to take part in coalition negotiations and to become a player in government. This was the second respect in which the electoral system boosted the SNP's chances, even if the prospect of office remained unlikely in the 1999 election. Labour's electoral strength and cordial relations with the Liberal Democrats – in Edinburgh and London – meant that the coalition between the two was widely anticipated. By 2003, however, relations between the two partners were a little more strained and there might have been an opening for the SNP had its own showing been stronger. That latter condition was fulfilled by 2007 and the party was a clear contender for office.

The Holyrood electoral system did not do its third kindness to the SNP until the 2011 election. In this case, it was the lack of proportionality that helped the party, which won a surprise majority of 53 per cent of seats based on 44 per cent of the vote in the regional list component. The SNP was not the first beneficiary of this 'winner's bonus': in 2003, the incumbent Labour and Liberal Democrats won a combined regional vote share of 41 per cent but were able to resume office having won 52 per cent of the seats. Two things combine to generate these skewed results: the preponderance of first-past-the-post seats means that there is often a lot of disproportionality to correct; and the fact that there are only seven seats per region means that there is limited scope for such correction in any one of those regions. If a party sweeps the constituency board within a region, it may already have more seats than it 'should' for proportionality, regardless of how the list seats are then allocated. All of this is a vivid illustration of how what may seem like the technical minutiae of politics can suddenly become very important. The surviving architects of devolution must have paused, as the 'Yes' poll rating crept upwards in the weeks before the referendum, to reflect on how events might have unfolded differently had they chosen a more purely proportional system.

Finally, devolution helped the SNP by creating a new and more distinctive Scottish political sphere. There was, of course, a Scottish political scene prior to devolution, just as there were separate Scottish institutions overseeing distinct legal and education systems, and administrative devolution with the Scottish Office within the Whitehall system of government headed by a Cabinet minister appointed by the Prime Minister. Nonetheless, devolution generated a new set of institutions within which the SNP would become a prominent operator. For instance, although there is no official opposition in the Scottish Parliament, the party's second place in the 1999 election entitled it by convention to the first two of the weekly First Minister's Questions. These were televised live, indicating a broader shift among the Scottish press and broadcast media towards coverage of the devolved political arena. Westminster politics were not forgotten by any means but had increasingly to share the limelight with events and personalities at Holyrood.

The enhanced visibility of Scottish politics was of course particularly useful for the SNP given its inevitably peripheral role at Westminster. It was not only during election campaigns that the party was sidelined as attention focused on the Labour–Conservative battle, with the Liberal Democrats in a supporting role at best. The adversarial institutions and culture at the UK level meant that, apart from occasional periods in the spotlight such as the SNP enjoyed in the 1970s, smaller parties were largely invisible in day-to-day politics.

By contrast, the SNP was the second biggest player in day-to-day politics in Scotland.

Being a Scottish-only party had its advantages in this new environment. For most SNP politicians, Holyrood was the chosen destination. Of the party's six MPs elected in 1997, all six – including Alex Salmond and John Swinney – then stood for the Scottish Parliament in 1999 and five of these stood down from Westminster at the 2001 election. (The exception was Salmond who, having stepped down as party chair by then, left the Holyrood spotlight to his successor Swinney.) By contrast, devolution rather exposed Scottish politicians from the Britain-wide parties as having their sights set on Westminster. If this seemed especially true of Labour, this does not necessarily mean that its key figures were likelier than senior Conservatives or Liberal Democrats to head to London. Labour was picked out instead because there were more Scottish Labour politicians in the first place and, being in government at Westminster, the party had some prominent roles to put them in. In any event, invidious comparisons were made between the overrepresentation of Scottish accents around the Cabinet table at Westminster and a perceived shortage of Labour talent at Holyrood. (See Table 4.1 in the next chapter for the voters' perspective on this.) More broadly, insofar as Scottish electoral politics was about which party would stand up for Scotland's interests against those of Westminster, the SNP leadership's preference for Edinburgh over London is likely to have worked to the party's reputational advantage.

FAILING TO PROFIT

As Table 3.1 has already indicated, however, any initial devolution dividend was limited. The party did at least benefit from its greater viability in Scotland-only contests: Figure 3.1, which tracks the party's vote share across the period 1997–2015, shows that a pattern immediately emerged whereby the SNP vote would increase in a Holyrood election but then slip back at the subsequent Westminster election. This pattern was, if anything, becoming more pronounced until it was abruptly interrupted by the extraordinary outcome in 2015. While we can only infer that this is a viability effect from the graph, the 2007 Scottish Election Study provided some

FIGURE 3.1: SNP CONSTITUENCY VOTE SHARES IN
UK AND SCOTTISH ELECTIONS, 1997–2015

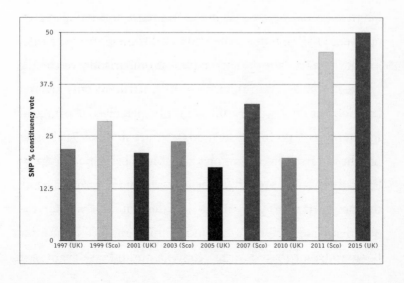

more direct evidence. Respondents were asked whether they
would have voted differently had this been a Westminster
election and, if so, why. Of those who had voted SNP but
would have gone another way in a general election, 55 per
cent reported that this was because their preferred party
'has no chance of forming a Westminster government' (Johns
et al., 2010, pp. 110–11).

But the graph also shows that the SNP was by no means
guaranteed a good showing even in Scottish-only contests.
After a strong start in 1999, the party slumped to 24 per
cent of the constituency and only 21 per cent of the list vote
in 2003. With support for independence no higher and support for the SNP on the slide, there were even fears within
the party – and hopes among its opponents – that devolution
might be able to live up to George Robertson's 1995 predic-
tion that it would 'kill nationalism stone dead'. In a more
temperate assessment, Edinburgh academic Lindsay Paterson
described the SNP in this period as 'becalmed' (2006, p. 46).
This was at an inopportune time, too, because Table 3.1
reveals Labour already to have been vulnerable in 2003.
It, too, had lost significant ground – indeed, its regional
list share was no higher in 2003 than in 2007 when it lost
power. But the SNP was unable to capitalise this time around.
Elsewhere in this book, we discuss some of the internal party
reasons why, regardless of the outside context, the SNP was
not in strong electoral form during this period. This chapter
is more about that external context, though, and why not

all of the supposed advantages of devolution for the party were materialising.

One reason is that these things take time. It was Ron Davies, former Welsh Secretary, who coined the description of devolution as 'a process, not an event' (Davies, 1999). But it was no less applicable to Scotland, especially given the form that devolution took in this case. While the Scotland Act of 1998 gave the Scottish Parliament the authority to legislate in all areas not explicitly reserved at Westminster, this was a transfer of the *potential* power to allow policy to diverge on either side of the border. It demarcated the areas into which those in power at Holyrood could reach for powers over time. So the Scottish executive (as the government at Holyrood was initially called) became slowly more powerful as the devolved institutions first bedded in and then began to flex their muscles.

Devolution is also a psychological process. It was not just about the Scottish institutions doing more but about this being noticed by politicians in the rest of the UK, by news editors, by commentators, and by voters. That was a pre-condition for the refocusing on the Scottish arena from which the SNP stood to profit. And that change in habits and priorities takes time too. Of course, it can be chivvied along, as by the SNP's decision on its election as a minority administration in 2007 to rename the executive as the Scottish government. By levelling the terminological playing field, this encouraged observers to see the Westminster

and Holyrood governments as two actors worthy of equal
attention. Whether this reflects either *de jure* or *de facto*
reality is immaterial; perceptions are what drive voters'
thinking and choices.

The psychological process of devolution is clearly visible in
trends documented by the Scottish Social Attitudes series and
set out in Table 3.2. The first is based on a general question
asking, 'Which institution do you think has the most influence over the way Scotland is run?' Respondents could also
select local councils or the European Union but, since few did
so and since our main interest is in the comparison between
Scottish and UK governments, we confine the comparison to
those. The table shows a clear and fairly steady increase in
the proportion choosing the Scottish government, up from
only one in six in 2000 to half of the electorate in 2011.

TABLE 3.2 TRENDS IN PERCEIVED IMPORTANCE OF SCOTTISH
         AND UK ARENAS, 2000–2011

	2000	2001	2003	2004	2005	2006	2007	2009	2010	2011
Scottish government	16	19	21	28	33	39	37	46	45	50
UK government	84	81	79	72	67	61	63	54	55	50
Scottish govern-ment policies		22	36	38	40	48	43	53	46	45
UK government policies		78	64	62	60	52	57	47	54	55

Source: UK Data Service, Scottish Social Attitudes Survey, 1999–2011

Reinforcing the point made above, it may not be coincidence that the biggest step change comes between 2007 and 2009 when the question wording changed from the 'Scottish Executive' to the 'Scottish Government'. Separate questions asked about whether changes in standards of health, education and living in Scotland over the previous year were mainly the result of the UK government's or the Scottish government's policies (or some other reason – again excluded from analysis here). We averaged responses across the three domains to create the second series in the table. Again, recognition of the Scottish government's impact started from a low base but built over time. Even when the increase was reversed in 2010, almost certainly by the macroeconomic and fiscal crises which were probably seen as limiting Holyrood's influence over living standards in particular, the balance between the two was still close to 50:50. Nonetheless, it is clear many voters took time to be convinced that the devolved institutions wielded significant powers and influence.

Psephologists are accustomed to distinguish between 'first-order' elections, typically those electing the national government, and 'second-order' elections to a range of other bodies that are deemed either subservient to or in some other way less important than that government. For English voters, this is clear-cut: Westminster elections are first-order arena while local and European elections are second-order. For Welsh and especially Scottish voters since devolution, things became less straightforward. Initially, Scottish Parliament elections always seemed likely to fall somewhere between the two (reflecting the fact that 'first-' and 'second-order' was always a continuum masquerading as a dichotomy). On the one hand, prima facie the devolved institutions were appreciably more powerful than, say, local councils. On the other hand, the figures towards the left-hand side of Table 3.2 make clear that there were plenty of Scots unconvinced about the importance of these elections. Understanding how voters reacted to this perceived unimportance helps us to explain the SNP's failure to reap much of an early devolution dividend.

One attractive option for voters at a second-order election is to take a 'free hit' against the first-order government. Since this meant Tony Blair's Labour for the first three devolved elections, it should have been good news for the SNP and indeed the party did make some ground at the expense of Labour in 1999. Yet Blair and New Labour remained popular in the early years of devolution. Additionally, at that time – that is, when devolved government was being anticipated rather than experienced – there were optimistic expectations about the powers of the new Scottish institutions (see Park and McCrone, 2006, pp. 17–18) and so Paterson et al. dispute that 'the election was seen as a chance to cast a risk-free protest vote against the incumbent Westminster government. Rather, voters revealed that what they are looking for in a Scottish election are parties that are willing to use the devolved institutions to promote Scotland's interests'

(2001, p. 44). The problems for the SNP arose when, having concluded that Westminster remained a good deal more important, voters saw the 2003 election as what John Curtice called 'a chance to experiment' (2006) with smaller parties. The upshot is in Table 3.1: 23 per cent of the regional list vote and seventeen seats going to the Greens, the Scottish Socialist Party and an array of other smaller parties. Having been a big loser in this surge of the minor parties, the SNP took little pleasure in the resulting 'rainbow parliament'.

The argument that an inclination to protest worked against the SNP in 2003 might sound strange given that there had been a protest element to its vote in Westminster elections ever since the 1960s – an element that would be visible again in 2015. But in devolved elections the SNP was a major party, not a riskless channel of protest. We mentioned earlier a survey question put to 2007 SNP voters who reported that they would have voted a different way had this been a general election. Only a quarter of these described 'sending a message to London' as one of the motivations for their SNP vote.

The party was thus falling between two stools in the early years of devolution. As the second force in Scottish politics, it did not offer the kind of pure protest option that was popular in 2003. But, if these protests served to strip the larger parties down to their cores, that left the SNP a long way adrift in second place. One consequence of the party's poor showing in 2003 was that an element inside the SNP interpreted the result as a need for a bolder approach, following the more anti-establishment route that had been offered by the Greens, Scottish Socialist Party and others who had won a significant presence in Holyrood. Criticism focused on John Swinney and the charge that he and others in the SNP leadership were modelling the SNP on New Labour. Bill Wilson, a relatively unknown party member, stood against Swinney for the leadership, highlighting the ease with which a challenge could be made to an incumbent leader. Swinney won 84 per cent of the vote but criticisms continued to be voiced. Campbell Martin, who had been elected as an SNP MSP in 2003, had been a strong supporter of Wilson's challenge and was expelled from the party a year later after attacking Swinney in the run-up to the European Parliament elections.

Swinney's challengers bemoaned what they saw as the party's downplaying of independence, which remained the basis of the SNP's core vote. Yet this was a policy that showed no sign of gaining support and was certainly no basis for populist protest votes. Another feature of early Scottish Parliament elections was that voters used them to register their views on devolution itself and, to the SNP's disadvantage, on whether independence should follow. Summing up the 2003 contest, John Curtice concludes that 'what the election outcome reflected most clearly was where people stood on Scotland's longstanding constitutional debate' (2006, p. 107). In other words, voters were still focused on whether there should be a Scottish government rather than on who best to do the job.

For the reasons made clear in Table 3.2, this slowly changed. Scottish governments started to do more and be seen to do more. More specifically, by the second term of the Scottish Parliament the Labour–Lib Dem coalition was developing a record on which it could be judged. Analyses of vote choice in 2003 and 2007 provide a telling comparison: in 2003, assessments of the UK government's performance proved more influential than assessments of the Scottish government's performance (Curtice, 2006); four years later, that pattern had reversed (Johns et al., 2010, pp. 113–14). Scottish elections were becoming more first-order or, put another way, more like normal elections – occasions for assessing the incumbent government and scrutinising its challengers.

This was, on the whole, a positive trend for the SNP, which was obviously a more plausible option for government in Scotland than in the UK as a whole, and which more generally stood to benefit the more that political attention was focused on a strengthening Scottish sphere rather than on Westminster. But a first-order Scottish arena, while a necessary condition for SNP electoral progress, would not in itself usher the party into office. We suggested earlier that the SNP in devolved elections was too big to be seen as a protest party but too far adrift to emerge as a governing party. Even when we consider the coalitional nature of government formation in the early period of devolution, the SNP was still between those two stools: too big to be a junior partner but too small to be the senior partner. Even if the arithmetic changed such that a Labour–SNP alliance would be less of a 'grand' and more of a standard coalition, relations between the two parties – hardly warm prior to devolution – were unlikely to improve given they were fighting for the same votes. The Lib Dems had become the natural party of coalition: their support was sufficiently different from Labour's, whereas the Tories would be politically toxic as partners. The SNP thus risked becoming the 'natural party of opposition' within the Scottish party system. Changing the terms of electoral trade required the party at least to get close to Labour, if not to overtake them.

HOW TO WIN A NORMAL ELECTION

Over the next two chapters, we examine how the SNP went from its rather dismal showing in 2003 to a majority in 2011, doubling its vote in the process. Vital in this success was the party's recognition, before many academics and commentators and indeed before its rival parties, that Scottish elections would increasingly resemble 'normal' or general elections and would be won or lost on the same basis. Before describing the SNP's specific approach in those upcoming chapters, we conclude this one by setting out the key features of an increasingly first-order Scottish electoral battleground. Put crudely, we need to know the game the

SNP had to play, and how that game has changed over the years, in order better to understand how the party won it.

'Class is the basis of British party politics; all else is *embellishment* and detail.' That was Peter Pulzer's (1967, p. 98) much-quoted summary of voting behaviour in post-war Britain. But the line was already overstated by the time it was published in 1967. In the same year, Winnie Ewing won the SNP's breakthrough by-election in Hamilton on a 38 per cent swing from Labour. Pulzer might have filed this under embellishment or detail but it was an early demonstration of the vulnerability of a class-based party – even on its own socioeconomic home turf. Today, while the outlines of class politics are still visible and many policy disputes have at least an implicit class component, the embellishment and detail have largely taken over. Certainly the proportion of voters whose choices can be predicted on the basis of their social class has declined sharply over the decades since the 1960s.

Some believe that this is because voters' class positions have become less clear-cut due to a range of societal changes: the decline of manufacturing industries and the resulting decline in blue-collar union membership; the sale of council housing and the rise in home ownership; and the growth in higher education and female employment leading to more mixed-class families. Others point out that the proportion of voters who regard themselves as belonging to a particular social class has not declined over the years, and instead

argue that it is the parties which severed the class-voting
link (Evans and Tilley, 2012), either by pursuing policies that
went against the interests of their class base or by eschew-
ing class-based appeals in favour of phrases empty enough to
appeal across the board, like 'hard-working families'. There
is probably something in both accounts, and we have no
need to climb off that fence because both imply the same
conclusion: an opening for the SNP in the electoral market.
The sociological changes eroded what had been the most
fertile soil for Labour voting, and already by 1992 there
were clear signs of SNP progress at the expense of Labour
among manual workers and union members (Bennie et al.,
1997, pp. 99–101). And the major parties' wish to downplay
the politics of class identity was obviously to the advantage
of a party seeking cross-class appeal based on the politics of
national identity. Not surprisingly, given the context as
described by Pulzer, commentators' initial reaction to the
1970s rise of the SNP was to remark on its ability to win
votes from across all classes (Miller, 1981; McCrone, 1992).
This ability equipped the party well for the changing electoral marketplace. We will see in Chapter 8 that cross-class
support would remain a hallmark of the SNP electorate some
forty years later.

Closely related to the decline of class voting was the
weakening of party loyalties. During the 1950s, each of
the two major parties not only used to win well over 40 per
cent of the vote but could count on doing so because so

many voters felt strong allegiances to 'their' party. These allegiances had often been inherited from parents, too – partisanship was learned at home but then reinforced at work. Identification with Labour became an integral part of the working-class and often largely Catholic communities based around heavily unionised industries in the west of Scotland. It is therefore easy to see how the social changes described above would have led to a decline not only in Labour voting but also in enduring loyalty to the party. Again, there are additional explanations based on party behaviour. An example is Labour's shift to the left during the early 1980s, which, according to Ivor Crewe, opened up an 'ideological chasm' between the party and its supporters and led to a significant weakening of Labour identification.

Whatever the causes, the result is the same. Figure 3.2 shows changes over the past fifty years or so in the proportions of BES Scottish respondents describing themselves as 'very strong', 'fairly strong' or 'not very strong' supporters of a particular party and the proportion reporting no identification with any party. The darker the shading, the stronger the identification, and the pattern is clear: the strength of partisan attachments has been in inexorable decline since the 1960s. There was a small upturn in 2010 (perhaps because a close race got partisan juices flowing) but still the proportion of very strong identifiers is barely a third of what it was in 1964 and, by 2010, around half of Scottish voters were reporting at most a leaning.

FIGURE 3.2: STRENGTH OF PARTY IDENTIFICATION IN SCOTLAND
AT UK GENERAL ELECTIONS, 1964–2010

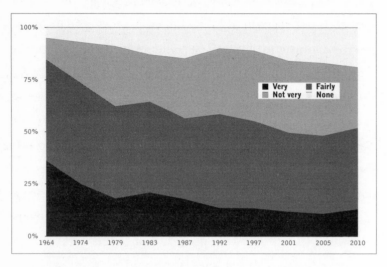

Source: British Election Study series, 1964–2010.
(N.B. The Scottish sample size in 2015 was too small for reliable estimates.)

This eroding of party loyalties was another profoundly
helpful development for the SNP. The party lacked the historical, sociological and religious roots of Labour and the
Conservatives and so did not have the kind of loyalist base
that in effect gave these parties – especially Labour, as time
went on – a significant head start in each election. As party
loyalties weakened, these head starts began to shorten. The
votes of 'very strong' identifiers can be more or less taken
for granted but the votes of 'not very strong' identifiers and
of course non-identifiers are up for grabs. Winning therefore
requires more than mobilising a core vote; it is about building a coalition of support each time around. In this context,

as the SNP would show during its surge to a majority at
Holyrood, parties can achieve major swings not only between
elections but even during a short election campaign.

Alongside these trends of class and partisan dealignment, a
third feature of today's British elections is ideological convergence. Labour's shift to the centre under Tony Blair not only
narrowed the gap between Labour and the Conservatives but,
in a Scottish context, more or less eliminated any differences
between Labour, the SNP and the Liberal Democrats. Figure
3.3 shows how BES respondents in Scotland placed themselves
and the four main parties across three elections for which the

FIGURE 3.3: AVERAGE VOTER SELF- AND PARTY PLACEMENTS
ON THE LEFT–RIGHT SCALE, 1997–2015

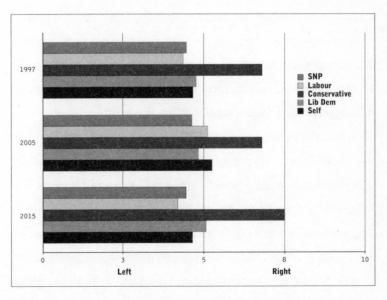

Source: Scottish Election Survey, 1997; British Election Studies, 2005, 2015

data are available, and confirms this convergence. Only the Conservatives offer anything particularly distinctive and so, for the majority of Scottish voters who seem to reject that option by default, there is very little meaningful choice available.

The fact of ideological convergence is not in itself necessarily helpful for the SNP. True, New Labour did help the SNP to present itself as the left-wing option in Scotland without having to make the kind of move in that direction that would alienate its more moderate voters. And for various reasons – discussed in detail in Chapter 8 – it is striking that voters in 2015 perceived so little shift to the left by the post-referendum SNP. But the more important point here is about the nature of political competition in Scotland given that there has consistently been so much agreement on the broad direction of policy. One point is that the constitutional question became more influential over voting decisions, exactly because it was the one major area in which the leading contenders were divided. Otherwise, however, where social democratic consensus reigned, electoral politics ceased to be about disagreement and instead became about which party was more likely to deliver agreed objectives. This is known as the valence or 'performance politics' model of voting. It is set out by Harold Clarke and colleagues (2004, 2009), who also make a compelling case for its relevance in recent British general elections.

The recipe for winning elections implied by the valence model is a simple one. Incumbents need to be seen to perform well; challengers need to persuade voters that they would perform better. For incumbents, economic performance usually takes centre stage – 'it's the economy, stupid' is a quintessentially valence model of voting – but 'performing well' also simply means avoiding pitfalls and crises. For challengers, things are more complicated because the assessment of likely performance is harder than judging a record in office. People are easier to judge than parties and so voters often rely heavily on their views of a party's leader – if he or she seems capable and decisive, the party will get some reflected credit. And parties themselves can project an image of competence by maintaining unity, downplaying unpopular or extreme positions, and avoiding what appear to be unrealistic promises. This lays out the task ahead of the SNP as it sought to replace Labour as Scotland's party of government. The following chapters describe how the task was achieved.

CHAPTER 4

RETURN OF THE KING

Alex Salmond was first elected to the Commons in 1987 when he took Banff and Buchan for the SNP from the Conservatives. It was the only Scottish seat at that election in which Labour's share of the vote declined. Salmond joined two 'retreads': Margaret Ewing, who won neighbouring Moray having been MP for East Dunbartonshire between 1974 and 1979, and Andrew Welsh in East Angus, who had also held that seat during the 1974–79 period. Later that year, Salmond stood successfully for the deputy leadership of his party and went on to contest the leadership against Ewing in 1990. Salmond won 77 per cent of delegates' votes, confounding media expectation at the start of the campaign that Ewing would win. But there was strong opposition to Salmond within the SNP. Gordon Wilson chose his moment to stand down as leader in a way designed to help Ewing. Jim Sillars, previously close politically to Salmond, came out for Ewing, as did a number of others on the left including in the '79 Group, a faction of the party's mainly younger figures committed to socialism and republicanism alongside independence. The conventional wisdom at the time was that, while Ewing was more popular as a person, Salmond was thought better equipped to offer a future.

SNP leaders often serve long stretches. By 1990, Wilson had been in post since 1979. Billy Wolfe before him had led the SNP for the decade from 1969. In contrast, Salmond's detractors inside the SNP responded to his election by predicting that he would not last a year. But by the time he stood down as leader a decade later, respect and even affection for Salmond had grown inside his party. He proved to be a transformative leader and, even had he not returned to the leadership in 2004, he would have already secured a place in the SNP's history as its most significant and successful leader until that point. His main achievement was to move his party from a suspicion of devolution to its embrace. This had been a difficult journey, as Chapter 6 describes. But he eventually united the party in support of the idea, and in doing so reduced the likelihood that the SNP would be portrayed merely as a wrecker in the new Scottish parliamentary elections.

The SNP's roots lay outside Parliament and it relied on its leaders giving their time and efforts while pursuing their jobs and careers. None of its leaders had the kind of wealth that would have allowed them the luxury of political engagement as a full-time hobby. While the SNP may have been small in comparison to other parties for most of its history, the lack of full-time elected politicians and related resources left the leadership with a heavier administrative burden than in other parties. The consequence was that the load was shared across a collective leadership. Moreover, the SNP had a suspicion of leaders and its early self-governing, participatory ethos entrenched the idea of collective leadership. The party formally had a chair, later styled a convenor, rather than a leader. When the party first emerged onto the scene with seven and then eleven MPs in 1974, it had leaders in both London and Scotland, and little thought had gone into the relationship between the two. The collective nature of leadership was evident in a rare poll in February 1981 asking voters to name the main leaders of the SNP. Gordon Wilson – the party's national chair – was named by 13 per cent of voters (including 26 per cent of SNP supporters), 18 per cent named Winnie Ewing (21 per cent of SNP supporters) and 28 per cent named Margo MacDonald (29 per cent of SNP supporters). The latter had lost her place as senior vice-chair (effectively deputy leader) in the party eighteen months previously, although she had assumed a prominent and very public leadership role in that capacity until voted out at the party conference in 1979 (Mitchell, 1996, p. 229).

Over time, the party added vice-chairs/convenors with particular responsibilities in response to new or growing pressures, thus widening the leadership further. Annual contests for national office were not only a means of gauging shifts of opinion inside the party but also provided an opportunity for budding politicians, denied much prospect of becoming MPs, to enter the political stage. Being a vice-chair/convenor provided a platform. Alex Salmond's early step into the political limelight came with his election as vice-chair for publicity in 1985, a role he defined in broad terms. On becoming SNP convenor in 1990, Salmond showed little interest in the party's internal organisational structure and assumed a role as leader that differed from predecessors. He saw the convenorship as much more like the leadership of other parties but was happy to operate within the existing structures. Ironically, it was his successor John Swinney, instinctively more collegiate in his style of leadership, who decided that the party should reduce the number of national office holders and formalise the role of leader. He recognised that devolution made the old collective approach redundant: the party convenor now had to be in Holyrood and to lead a larger contingent of parliamentarians than in the past. Swinney's personality meant that few would notice much difference in style as a consequence of the changing rules. However, they meant that Salmond would formally become party leader when he took over in 2004. He would be a high-profile leader who would come to command his party.

'ALEX SALMOND FOR FIRST MINISTER':
AN ELECTORAL ASSET

Leaders matter for voters' choices. This claim, not ostensibly controversial, was until quite recently questioned by many psephologists (see, for example, King, 2002; Curtice and Holmberg, 2005). That was partly because election campaigning and coverage used to be far less 'presidentialised' than it is now. The arrival of televised debates in UK elections only intensified the tendency for leaders to be paraded on TV in a way that would have shocked those brought up on postwar election campaigns. But it was also because it was thought that assessments of leaders merely reflected existing allegiances to the parties that they led. If those who already supported the SNP were bound to like Alex Salmond, while those with other allegiances were bound to dislike him, then there was little scope for leaders to swing anyone's vote.

Those who doubted the electoral importance of leaders were probably always more sceptical than they should have been (and were helped to remain so because those who didn't believe in leader effects tended not to look for them). Such scepticism is certainly misplaced now that, as discussed at the end of the previous chapter, many voters have no strong partisan loyalty. Most still lean towards a particular party (and away from another) but they do not lean very far. To modify the sentence that ended the previous paragraph, then: while a minority of the strongly partisan are more or less *bound* to like or dislike a certain leader, a larger group of voters are only inclined to do so. And these inclinations can be overridden. Recent studies of voting in UK general elections have highlighted Tony Blair's capacity to win votes from those not predisposed to vote Labour, and Ed Miliband's capacity to lose votes from among those who were thus predisposed (Evans and Andersen, 2003; BES, 2015). In both cases, voters reached judgements about these leaders that were independent of – and that prevailed over – their partisan sympathies.

If the key to a leader's influence is that she is evaluated distinctly from her party, then that influence is at its greatest in cases where leaders might be said to 'rise above' party. This is usually achieved through a combination of longevity and force of personality, two boxes conspicuously ticked in the case of Alex Salmond. Indirect evidence of this comes from his very high levels of name recognition. Those sufficiently interested in politics to, say, be reading this book might be startled at the proportions of voters who have not heard of even high-ranking politicians. Those proportions will be still higher in the case of those based at Holyrood, who are often eclipsed in media coverage that focuses on Westminster. Partly because of his long first stint as SNP leader, and partly because of his high media profile (including three appearances on *Have I Got News For You* between 1995 and 1999), Salmond has generally been far more familiar to Scottish voters than have his rivals. An August 2008 YouGov poll asked voters to report their familiarity with various Scottish politicians. Only 2 per cent reported never having heard of Alex Salmond, compared to 10 per cent for Nicola Sturgeon, 15 per cent for Annabel Goldie (by then three years into her tenure as Scottish Conservative leader) and 45 per cent for Iain Gray (the eventual winner of the Scottish Labour leadership contest that was in progress at the time of the poll). Moreover, 48 per cent claimed to 'know a lot about' Salmond, compared to 28 per cent, 19 per cent and 4 per cent for Sturgeon, Goldie and Gray respectively. By a year into his First Ministership, then, Alex Salmond was by far the best-known politician in the Scottish arena. Another YouGov poll in 2008 asked voters: 'If Scotland became a republic in the next few years and chose its own President, who would you prefer?' and gave them three options: 'A non-political figure; Some other political leader; Alex Salmond'. The fact that Salmond came third in that poll is less relevant here than the fact that he was singled out as a category in himself.

In such cases, the pattern anticipated by those psephologists – that voters would simply judge the leader by his or her party – may be reversed. People may project the characteristics of a well-known leader onto a less familiar or a changing party. The widespread misconception among the commentariat (corrected by Ford and Goodwin, 2014) that UKIP was a party of the blazer-wearing, putter-wielding middle classes was doubtless driven in large part by the prominence of Nigel Farage in the party's rise. Lacking detailed information about the party, pundits judged it by its leader. Voters will do the same. The SNP is a more familiar party than UKIP but Salmond's prominence means that his image still has the potential to colour that of his party.

So there are three broad ways in which a leader can be an electoral asset – or liability. The first is through simple like-ability. Charles Kennedy is a good example of a leader who won votes for his party not because he was widely regarded as the best option for Prime Minister but because he scored highly on personal popularity (Evans and Andersen, 2005). The second is through respect. Margaret Thatcher was never widely liked (and might not have relished *Have I Got News For You*) but her reputation for decisiveness, honesty and effective leadership extended far beyond her Conservative support base (Mughan, 2000). Both of these can be described as direct effects of leadership: that is, voters making decisions based on the personal characteristics – whether explicitly political or otherwise – of the party leaders. However, there may also be indirect effects and this is the third way in which leaders can influence electoral outcomes. At the 1997 general election, Tony Blair scored well on likeability and was respected for a range of leadership traits like competence, effectiveness and caring. However, the direct effect of his personality accounted for only a small fraction of the surge in Labour's vote share (Bartle and Crewe, 2002). Harder to measure but almost certainly larger was the indirect effect of Blair on the image and expectations of the party through the abolition of Clause IV, the appeal to the aspirations of 'middle England', including promised restraint in spending and taxation, and the improvement in the party's reputation for competence in general and economic competence in particular. For every voter who was won over by Blair personally, several more were won over by Labour as refashioned by Blair. And, if the big question for doubters was 'just how new "New" Labour really *is*', then the simplest route to an answer was to judge the party by its suddenly dominant new leader.

When the SNP decided to use 'Alex Salmond for First Minister' rather than the party's name on the regional list ballot in 2007, then, they were seeking more than just an alphabetical advantage. By maximising Salmond's prominence, they were encouraging all three kinds of leader effects: capitalising on any advantage Salmond enjoyed in terms of both personal popularity and First Ministerial qualities, but also reminding voters that an SNP administration would be led by Salmond and could therefore be expected to evince those same qualities. In the rest of this chapter, we take a closer look at Salmond's potential for electoral influence under all three of those headings, and use election survey data to assess how far that potential was realised.

Likeability is gauged easily enough because a number of surveys have asked voters to rate Alex Salmond and other prominent figures on a scale from 0 ('strongly dislike') to 10 ('strongly like'). Table 4.1 shows Salmond's average ratings across four such surveys, and also indicates how far his rating

TABLE 4.1: SALMOND'S RATINGS RELATIVE TO OTHER LEADERS
ON 0–10 DISLIKE–LIKE SCALE

	MAY–JUNE 1997	APRIL 2007	APRIL 2011	AUGUST 2014
Alex Salmond	5.4	4.7	5.5	4.4
COMPARED TO HOLYROOD LEADERS				
Jack McConnell	—	+0.7	—	—
Annabel Goldie	—	+0.6	+1.2	—
Nicol Stephen	—	+0.4	—	—
Iain Gray	—	—	+1.5	—
Nicola Sturgeon	—	—	—	-0.3
COMPARED TO WESTMINSTER LEADERS				
Tony Blair	-1.2	+0.8	+2.0	—
John Major	+1.6	—	—	—
Gordon Brown	—	+0.2	+0.8	+0.4
David Cameron	—	+0.9	+2.4	+1.9
Ed Miliband	—	—	+1.4	—
Alistair Darling	—	—	—	+0.8
Nigel Farage	—	—	—	+1.7

Sources: Scottish Election Studies, 1997; Scottish Election Studies, 2007, 2011;
Scottish Referendum Study, 2014

was above (+) or below (-) those of his rivals at the time.
While there have been fluctuations in Salmond's popularity,
his mean rating has never drifted too far from 5, the neutral
point of the scale. This might sound a middling performance
but, once we bear in mind that voters do not typically find
politicians all that appealing (the average rating across all the
other leaders in the table is 4.1), a score around 5 starts to

look rather better. So Alex Salmond is at least relatively likeable. This is underlined by the glut of '+' signs in the table. Salmond was invariably more popular than his rival leaders at Holyrood, quite strikingly so by 2011, and also usually more popular than the other major players on the UK scene.

The exceptions are instructive. First, even at the peak of his popularity in 2011, Salmond was never close to the ratings (among Scottish voters) of Tony Blair in 1997. This is not because Blair was more widely adored: the proportions choosing the highest point on the scale were roughly the same (21 per cent for Blair in 1997, 20 per cent for Salmond in 2011). It is because Blair alienated far fewer voters: just 2 per cent were at the 'strongly dislike' extreme, compared to 18 per cent for Salmond. The SNP's leader was by that time a relatively popular but also a polarising figure.

This is largely because the SNP takes a clear position on the constitution that is bound to provoke opposition in some quarters. As the example of Blair highlights, tactics for avoiding strong voter distaste include policy moderation and the accommodation of public opinion. The SNP's longstanding commitment to independence, a radical and polarising stance, was always likely to prove very unpopular with at least some voters. And the toll taken on Salmond's likeability by the referendum campaign underscores the point. It is not that his personality changed much between 2011 and 2014; rather, his opponents felt more strongly about what he was doing. By the referendum, Salmond was 'strongly disliked' by 31 per cent of the Scottish electorate, and that is one reason – discussed further in Chapter 7 – why it made sense to give way to Nicola Sturgeon, the only other example in the entire table of a politician more popular than Salmond at any given point.

Another reason for the polarised opinions on Salmond is just how long he has been on the scene. There is a natural tendency for attitudes to strengthen over time, driven by people's psychological motivation to defend their existing opinions (Lodge and Taber, 2000). If Salmond's fans recognise his successes and ignore or explain away his missteps, while his detractors do the opposite, the effect is a slow centrifugal shift towards the extremes on the 0–10 likeability scales. Figure 4.1 below shows that this is exactly

FIGURE 4.1: CHANGING DISTRIBUTION OF ATTITUDES
TOWARDS ALEX SALMOND, 1997 AND 2011

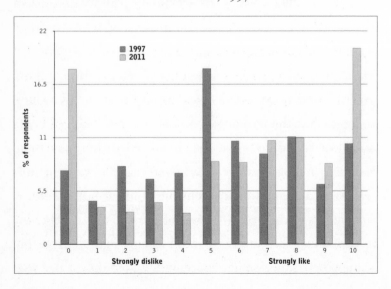

what happened between 1997 and 2011. The distribution for 1997, with its obvious peak at the neutral point on the scale, is anything but that of a 'love him or hate him' politician. By 2011, though, Salmond was more familiar, more voters had made up their minds about him and the effect on the profile of opinion is clear. Again, it is questionable how much his personality changed over this period. The change was in voters' reactions.

Our argument so far might be taken to imply that any leader of the SNP who stuck around as long as Alex Salmond would polarise opinion in the same way. There is some truth in this but we do not mean to discount the possibility that there is also something specifically Marmite-ish in Salmond's political persona. Table 4.2 shows the results of three opinion poll questions – the first two from August 2007 and the third from January 2012 – in which respondents were asked to choose from a list the single quality or trait that they would most associate with Alex Salmond. We have classified these qualities under broad headings in order to make those polls as comparable as possible. The resulting table may look complex but the patterns are clear enough. Salmond gets credit for friendliness and even in some cases for charisma. Humility is not a strong suit, however. Large proportions saw arrogance and condescension as his dominant traits. The figures in the first two rows of Table 4.2 go a long way to explaining the pattern for 2011 in that Figure 4.1 graph. Some voters saw a genial figure with whom they could well imagine going for a drink. Others saw an arrogant figure who would talk down to them throughout that drink, and were appalled at the prospect.

TABLE 4.2: QUALITIES MOST ASSOCIATED WITH ALEX SALMOND
IN 2007 AND 2012 POLLS

	YOUGOV, AUG '07	%	YOUGOV, AUG '07	%	SURVATION, JAN '12	%
ARROGANCE	Arrogant	28	Patronising	32	Arrogant	34
	Humble	1				
LIKEABILITY	Friendly	21			Charismatic	6
	Unfriendly	1				
HONESTY			Honest	31	Honest	7
			Dishonest	5	Opportunist	17
STRENGTH			Strong	28	Competent	13
					Statesman	12
			Weak	3		
IDEAS/ INTELLIGENCE	Bad ideas for Sco	11			Intelligent	11
	Good ideas for Sco	37				
TOTALS		100		100		100

Since perceived arrogance is Salmond's most obvious vulnerability in personality terms, it is worth adding a couple more points about it. One is to question the notion that this explains Salmond's 'women problem' – insofar as there is one. The conventional wisdom among Salmond's accusers here is set out by David Torrance: 'He's quite aggressive and assertive, verging on arrogance. That's obviously not going to resonate very well with female voters' (Goldhill, 2014). This seemed to be underlined in June 2015 when Salmond told Anna Soubry, Conservative junior minister, to 'behave yourself, woman' during a parliamentary debate. While not quite the 'calm down, dear' for which David Cameron was similarly accused of sexism, this will have done nothing to dent Salmond's reputation for condescension. However, while the polling data confirm that voters have noted the arrogance, the assumption (far from unique to Torrance) that this is a particular problem among female voters remains just that – an assumption. One simple way of testing it is to compare men's and women's responses to the Survation poll question from Table 4.2. It turns out that Salmond is seen primarily as arrogant by 31 per cent of women – and 37 per cent of men. Not only were women less likely to complain of arrogance but they were also more likely to regard him as honest and charismatic. This is hard to square with the notion that Salmond's personality is a particular turn-off for women.

This dubious conventional wisdom about Salmond and women reflects two tendencies in commentary on gender and politics. First, it is always women who are judged to be the aberrant group, whose opinions or behaviour need special attention or explanation. Even when opposition to independence was clearly the majority position among both sexes, and so hardly a pathology to be explained, a Scottish Centre for Social Research report (Ormston, 2013) asked, 'Why don't more women support independence?' rather than wondering why so many men do. Second, there is heavy reliance on the psychology of personality and emotions, with the relationship between male politicians and female voters often treated as a kind of courtship. (An exact-phrase Google search for 'woo female voters' yields several thousand hits, compared to 'woo male voters' which attracts eighty-eight.)

All of this would be more forgivable were there not a straightforward political explanation for a gender gap in Salmond's popularity. As that report showed, independence was markedly more popular among men throughout his tenure as First Minister and, as discussed further in Chapter 8, this also translated into a persistent gender gap in support for and membership of the SNP (see also Johns et al., 2012). It is hardly surprising that the leader – for twenty of the past twenty-five years – of a party committed to independence would prove more likeable for those who support that policy. So, insofar as women have a particular problem with Alex Salmond, it is likely to have had more to do with policy than personality.

The second point to make about arrogance is that, while it might not be very likeable, it probably does little to erode respect, and respect is the second of the key ways in which a leader affects voting. David Cameron is another example of a leader widely regarded as arrogant. His percentage for that trait among British respondents in the 2012 Survation poll was 34 per cent, the same as Salmond's among Scottish respondents, but this did not mean he was not an electoral asset to his party. And Table 4.2 contains ample evidence of other sources of public respect, grudging or otherwise, for Salmond's leadership. If we distinguish 'warmth' from 'strength' traits, the latter look a particularly long suit: Salmond scores well not only on strength itself but also on competence, intelligence and ideas.

While what it takes to be Prime or First Minister is to some extent in the eye of the beholder, it is hard to imagine that competence and decisiveness are not ranked highly by most voters. So it is no surprise that Alex Salmond performed very well in pre-election polls in 2007 and 2011 that asked voters who would make the best First Minister. Admittedly, the weakness of his main rivals, especially in 2011, helped to widen Salmond's advantage, but his leadership credentials were clearly established – including among an electorate that went beyond SNP supporters. Even judged in absolute rather than relative terms, as in mid-term polls asking whether voters were satisfied or dissatisfied with his performance in office, Salmond managed a net positive rating in every poll between 2007 and early 2014 (by which point voters were probably judging him less as First Minister and more as the leader of the 'Yes' campaign). Given that public assessments of politicians tend to the negative side, this is a striking statistic. Small wonder that the SNP wanted the prospect of 'Alex Salmond for First Minister' to be uppermost in voters' minds at the moment of decision.

While impressions of Salmond as a capable if cocksure

leader were formed a long time ago and have only crys-
tallised since, there is one area – integrity – in which his
image does seem to have changed over time. In March 2007,
YouGov asked: 'Leaving aside your views on who would
make the best First Minister, which of these do you regard as
generally trustworthy and untrustworthy?' With 34 per cent
naming him as trustworthy and 26 per cent as untrustworthy, Salmond was the only one of the five politicians named
whose rating was on balance positive. And Table 4.2 shows
that, later that same year, Salmond was overwhelmingly seen
as honest rather than dishonest. However, by 2012 only
7 per cent of respondents were associating Salmond primarily with honesty. Rather more were choosing 'opportunist',
which, while not exactly an antonym, has a less than trustworthy flavour to it. In February 2014, Salmond was named
by 32 per cent of Scots as the politician (from a list of ten)
that they trusted the least. Although this placed him behind
David Cameron, he was nevertheless far ahead of any other
Scottish politician.

Of course, as the referendum campaign heated up, there
was a large group of voters strongly inclined both to disbe-
lieve Salmond's claims and to see him in a negative light. So
it could be argued that the shift simply reflects the political
context rather than a decline in Salmond's perceived integrity per se. Yet the line between the two cannot be sharply
drawn, given, for example, the controversy over the existence
and content of legal advice about an independent Scotland's

EU membership. It is hard to believe that this did not take a toll on Salmond's credentials as a 'pretty straight sort of guy'. Nonetheless, a YouGov poll in March 2014 provided evidence that Salmond still retained credibility even among some opponents of independence. The question posed was: 'Thinking about the current debate over Scotland's future and the independence referendum, how much do you trust the statements and claims made by the following people?' In an increasingly febrile climate, every figure named was more distrusted than trusted. However, and at a time when the 'No' lead of 60–40 meant that a majority was predisposed not to trust pro-independence statements and claims, the trust gap was still narrower for Salmond than for any of the politicians on the Better Together side of the debate. Strikingly, this remained the case in late August 2014 when a parallel question also asked about Gordon Brown. Salmond was still regarded as the most trustworthy politician apart from one. The exception was Nicola Sturgeon.

What all of this establishes is that, if leaders can indeed have direct effects on voting behaviour, Alex Salmond certainly had the potential to win votes for his party. We have not yet established that that potential was realised. Demonstrating that leaders matter is difficult for the reason highlighted at the outset of this section, namely that opinions of a leader also reflect opinions of a party. It would be no surprise to learn that, of those who deem Alex Salmond to be the strongest candidate for First Minister at a given election, a large majority go on to vote SNP. But this does not mean that the leadership assessment drove the voting decision; it might just as well be that those who already liked the SNP for other reasons were also predisposed to think its leader the best option for First Minister. Identifying leader effects requires statistical analysis in which all of those predispositions are held constant. While that analysis itself can be as complex as its name, multivariate logistic regression, suggests, the underlying logic is quite simple. Effectively, the search is for pairs of people who share the same opinions of the SNP (its constitutional policy, its performance in office and so on) but who take a different view of Alex Salmond. If both individuals in the pair vote the same way, then those leadership opinions did not matter. But if the one who liked Salmond voted SNP while the more Salmond-sceptic voter did not, then that would suggest that leadership mattered more than those other factors.

Because it can disentangle the electoral effects of leadership from the effects of the myriad other things that might influence voters' decisions, regression also allows us to compare the importance of all these factors. Figure 4.2 is based on the Scottish Parliament election of 2011. Each bar in the chart represents the power of that factor to predict whether a voter chose the SNP on the constituency ballot in that election. (For those who prefer a more technical definition, it is provided in the label below the horizontal axis. We choose the constituency rather than the list vote here because, since

'Alex Salmond for First Minister' was the party's registered billing on the list ballot, using that might lead us to overstate the general importance of leadership on voting.)

FIGURE 4.2: THE EFFECT OF VARIOUS FACTORS ON THE LIKELIHOOD OF AN SNP CONSTITUENCY VOTE, 2011

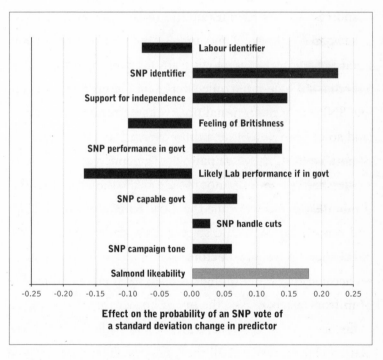

Effect on the probability of an SNP vote of
a standard deviation change in predictor

Source: Scottish Election Study, 2011

Not surprisingly, the single most potent factor was whether that voter was an SNP identifier – that is, reported them-selves as 'generally a supporter' of the party. If support for independence looks surprisingly unimportant, this is proba-bly because much of its effect is swallowed up in this party identification variable: the most likely reason for someone being a longstanding SNP identifier is support for independence, and so the constitutional variable in Figure 4.2 captures its effect only among non-loyalists. In the next chapter, we look in detail at how the SNP profited from the powerful electoral effect of its own record in government – and voters' less favourable impressions of how Labour would have performed. For present purposes the important bar is the one at the bottom. It confirms that opinions of Alex Salmond did indeed have a powerful and direct effect on voting choice at this election. Other things remaining the same (a simpler definition of what regression achieves statistically), those who liked Alex Salmond were a good deal more likely to vote SNP. Of course, the flip side of this is that those who disliked Salmond were a good deal *less* likely to vote SNP. The reason we know that he was ultimately a vote-gainer for his party is because voters' opinions about Salmond mattered *and* those opinions, as set out earlier, were on balance clearly favourable.

VOTING FOR SALMOND'S PARTY

Even if opinions of Alex Salmond were important in 2011, they were clearly very far from the whole story. Voters were influenced by their constitutional preferences, their national identity, their assessments of the parties' records and likely performance, the tones of the rival campaigns, and so on. This brings us back to the distinction between the direct and indirect effects of leadership. To the extent that Salmond's leadership enhanced the SNP's often favourable ratings on these various other criteria, then he will have had an indirect effect on voting in that election and, indeed, on opinions of the SNP throughout and beyond his time at the helm. There are two reasons to suspect that Salmond exerted particularly strong indirect effects of this kind. The first is simply his dominant position within the party, earned partly by force of personality but also by that redefinition of the role of leader described earlier. More or less by definition, a powerful leader is one able to bring the party's policies and priorities in line with his or her own. Insofar as voters then decide based on those policies and priorities, the leader has had an indirect effect. The second reason is the SNP's lack of any experience or record in office. Sarah Butt (2006) has shown that, when judging the economic competence of an opposition party, voters rely quite heavily on their assessments of the party's leader. That reliance is likely to be even heavier if the party is not only in opposition but has never been in government. So voters in the run-up to 2007, struggling to get a handle on the tyro SNP's capacity to govern, were likely to form a judgement based partly on the competence of its experienced leader. Even if Salmond had not governed Scotland, he had 'governed' his party, and voters could draw inferences – accurately or otherwise – from that.

We would pick out two general areas – competence (especially of the economic kind) and moderation – in which the SNP is likely to have benefited from being seen through the prism of Alex Salmond's leadership. The polling evidence surveyed above makes clear that Salmond was seen as a capable and decisive leader: desirable properties to rub off on a party. It is noteworthy that, when Labour's campaigning prophesied chaos and conflict should the SNP win, this was largely about relations between the Scottish and Westminster governments. Given Salmond's personality and leadership style, it was easier for opponents to suggest belligerence in his dealings with London than to expect weakness and disunity within an SNP government. It will surely also have helped, given the party's economic inexperience, that Salmond had a strong background in that field. While the devolved institutions had limited room for macroeconomic manoeuvre, there remained important questions about fiscal discipline. Moreover, the SNP had itself asserted that much could be done to improve competitiveness and economic growth even within the limited powers afforded by devolution, however much its ambitions were soon undermined by the global downturn that began shortly after the SNP came to power. Again, while the leadership of Salmond will not have entirely quelled doubts about the untested SNP's credentials in the economic field, it will at least have made disarray or disaster seem less likely.

Another way in which voters seem to judge competence

in general, and economic competence in particular, is moderation. When British voters in 1997 had to assess the macroeconomic trustworthiness of 'New' Labour, they might have been persuaded partly by Tony Blair's personal competence, but probably much more important was his having hauled New Labour to the ideological centre. While, unlike Blair, Salmond had further to travel than his party in order to reach that same destination, the story is otherwise similar: a leader becomes convinced of the virtues – especially electoral – of moderation and pursues that strategy to the point at which the voters cannot help noticing. In the previous chapter, we noted the Scottish public's perception of the SNP as a moderate party, leaning to the left – but only leaning. A YouGov poll in September 2015 showed that they have the same impression of Salmond. Asked to place him on a scale from left to right, voters' most common response was 'slightly left of centre' (and they placed him discernibly to the right of Nicola Sturgeon). Of course, there is projection to and fro here: some will have judged Alex Salmond by his party rather than vice versa. Nonetheless, given Salmond's own journey towards moderation and his dominant position, it was hard to see the SNP under his leadership lurching far from the centre-left ground that is the ideological mainstream in Scotland.

In the case of the SNP, however, moderation is less about left and right and more about the constitutional issue. Here, Salmond had long been a pragmatist. He was a consistent supporter of devolution at a time when the SNP adopted a much harder line on the issue and, as discussed in Chapter 6, slowly brought the party around to his view. If the pledge of a referendum on independence, the clearest sign of the party's own moderation on this issue, had been forced upon a leader obviously keener on a harder line, there would have remained major doubts about the immediate constitutional consequences of an SNP victory. Yet Salmond had instead obviously been in the vanguard of the party's strategic repositioning on independence. Naturally, in 2007 in particular, there remained doubts about whether the SNP's new-found moderation would persist beyond the election it was designed to win (similar to the 1997 doubts about whether the new administration would govern as 'New' Labour). By 2011, however, after four years of Salmond as First Minister and in clear command of his party, voters had reason to accept the authenticity of the SNP's apparent constitutional moderation based on Salmond's own restraint in that area.

That point about command of the party is crucial. Voters are much less likely to project a leader's moderation onto his or her party if there is vocal opposition to the approach within that party. So it wasn't only Salmond's own pragmatic position that mattered here. Insofar as his personality and popularity persuaded fellow parliamentarians and party activists to adopt gradualism without obvious internal conflict, the boost to the SNP's reputation both for moderation and for unity is likely to have paid electoral dividends.

Of course, nothing breeds harmony like success. Once the SNP's poll rating had overtaken Labour's by mid-2006, the party had more to lose from disunity, and given Salmond's prominence in that rise, more to thank its leader for. There is a virtuous circle of direct and indirect effects here. By being a more electorally attractive leader, Salmond was able to secure a position from which he could make the party more electorally attractive – and make electoral success a higher priority than it might have been to those of a more funda-mentalist orientation.

Results from the 2007 survey of SNP members (introduced in Chapter 2) illustrate this circle. When asked about their reasons for joining the party, those arriving since 2005 were disproportionately likely to refer to Alex Salmond himself – and disproportionately unlikely to mention independence (Mitchell et al., 2011, p. 81). The fact that Salmond was able to attract new members to the party is further suggestive of a direct electoral effect. If those new activists contributed to success in subsequent elections, then that is an obvious indirect effect of his leadership. And if those new mem-bers shifted the balance of opinion within the activist base towards the leadership's more gradualist approach, then that will have helped the party's electoral image too.

The front cover of the SNP's 2007 manifesto was a por-trait of Alex Salmond, seated on a desk in what looked like an executive's office and staring straight into the camera with as statesmanlike an expression as he could muster. Another full-page portrait, this time alongside Nicola Sturgeon, appeared opposite the first page of text, which mentioned health, policing and taxation before independence – and then only to reassure readers with that promise of a referendum. These opening pages are testament to Salmond's dominance within the party, the ascendancy of his pragmatic agenda and in particular his centrality to its electoral appeal. 'Think SNP, think Salmond' was a main plank of the party's electoral strategy, and this chapter has provided many reasons why it paid off.

CHAPTER 5

A SAFE PAIR OF HANDS

Elections are often reported as if the voters were of a
single mind. 'The electorate decided that it was time
for a change,' we might be told, as if the outcome was
decided by one impatient dictator. Of course, election outcomes
do not represent the collective will but the aggregation of mil-
lions of individual wills. It was not Scotland that decided that
the SNP should be the largest party in 2007, or should win an
outright majority in 2011. What happened was that, in contests that were widely (if to some extent misleadingly) billed as
a battle between the SNP and Labour for power in Holyrood,
enough voters preferred the SNP to deliver first a narrow and

then a thumping victory. In short: enough voters believed that the SNP was fit for office or, at least, more fit than Labour.

Not that everyone who voted SNP in these elections was focused on the party's likely performance in government. As described in Chapter 3, Scottish Parliament elections were also about expressing longstanding party loyalties or views on the big constitutional question. The SNP's base in these, and indeed any, elections was the substantial minority of Scottish voters who had long been convinced of the case for independence. But this cannot explain the big SNP gains that are the subject of this chapter. A simple graph (Figure 5.1) proves the point. While the SNP's vote share declined

FIGURE 5.1: TRENDS IN SUPPORT FOR INDEPENDENCE AND FOR THE SNP

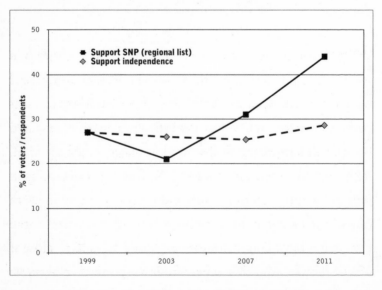

Sources: Election results and Scottish Social Attitudes Survey, 1999–2011

and then sharply improved, the percentage of Scottish voters favouring independence barely shifted. Whatever was causing fluctuations in the solid line, it was not the dashed line.

We argue that the 'whatever' was the perception of the SNP as a safe pair of governing hands. This perception initially had to be taken on trust, since the party had never held national office before. By 2011, after a term in minority government, the SNP had a record to defend, and it was a record that was viewed positively by most voters. In this chapter, we examine how the SNP first persuaded a growing number of Scots that the party was ready for office, and then governed in a way that won round many more voters.

AN UNEXPECTED VICTORY

If 'the electorate' was indeed a body with just one mind, then its overriding reaction to the SNP's victory in 2007 would probably have been surprise. The SNP's eventual largest-party status was achieved with little to spare, and few had been confident of the outcome in advance of the election. Although by late 2006 the party had overtaken Labour in Holyrood vote intention polls, and remained ahead in every one of the twelve polls during the last three months of the campaign, most commentators expected the gap to close if not to reverse. And this expectation had looked reasonable enough. For one thing, incumbents usually regain ground in the run-up to polling day. For another, Labour had won most votes and most seats in every Scottish nationwide election since 1945. Any defeat for Labour was in that sense bound to be a major shock.

Arguably, this was indeed a Labour defeat more than an SNP victory. The adage holds that 'oppositions don't win elections; incumbents lose them' and in this case two Labour incumbents were competing for the voters' disapproval: the Blair government at Westminster and the Scottish government led by Jack McConnell in which Labour were senior coalition partners alongside the Liberal Democrats. Performance ratings of both UK and Scottish Labour were appreciably into negative territory (Johns et al., 2010, p. 73). At the UK level, Tony Blair was close to both the end of his reign and the nadir of his popularity, with the 'cash for honours' scandal in full swing, the Iraq War dragging on, and the decision to replace Trident proving unpopular in Scotland. Scottish Labour's acquiescence on Trident and refusal to criticise action in Iraq contributed to a general impression that the party was under London's close supervision. So did the party's refusal to countenance any increase in powers for the Scottish Parliament, a stance more hardline even than that of the Scottish Conservatives. There were also domestic weaknesses in Scottish Labour's hand in 2007. Jack McConnell himself was not especially popular, even among his own party's supporters, and the party failed to impress many voters either with its record on key devolved issues like health and crime or with a conviction that it would stand up for Scotland in its dealings with Labour colleagues in Westminster.

Yet these problems – Iraq, lacklustre leadership at Holyrood, a feeling that Scottish Labour was in hock to the UK party – were not particularly new. Indeed, as Figure 5.1 shows, Labour had already been struggling to win over more than one in three Scottish voters back in 2003 – and even slipped below 30 per cent when it came to the regional list vote. It was the largest party more because of fragmented opposition than because of the staunchness of its support. The big change by 2007 was therefore not the slight slippage in the Labour vote but the big surge in the SNP vote. Perhaps the adage should be recast: incumbents won't lose elections until oppositions win them.

So how did the SNP make these gains? How did it convince what turned out to be just enough voters of its fitness for office, especially given its absence of any record in national government (and very limited experience even at local council level)? Apprehension over the SNP's likely performance in government ranged widely: there was the constitutional issue, general relations with the UK government, and everyday domestic politics – i.e. the handling of health, education, transport and the other devolved areas. On the constitutional question, basic parliamentary arithmetic should have eased voters' fears. No poll indicated the SNP coming anywhere near to winning a majority, and the other parties (aside from the Greens) were opposed not only to independence but to the referendum proposed by the SNP. Nonetheless, it was probably that referendum pledge – which, as discussed in Chapter 6, proved controversial within the party – that was more important in reassuring voters. It reduced the perceived risk of an SNP victory, defusing any 'vote SNP on Thursday, get independence on Friday' line of campaigning against the party. The commitment to a referendum also helped to foster an image of moderation.

The second question concerned day-to-day relations with Westminster. Even if the SNP could not hustle Scotland into independence, the party might pursue that aim by seeking conflict with London at every turn, either neglecting questions about devolved policy or simply using them to push its constitutional agenda. A central theme in Labour's campaign was that those relations with Westminster, harmonious under the Labour governments in London and Edinburgh, would become poisonous under an SNP government with an interest in constitutional conflict and instability. However, by 2007, what had been an advantage for Scottish Labour in 1999 and 2003 had turned into a disadvantage. The relationship with the party's Westminster government was seen as one of subservience rather than harmony – as in the jibe about 'London Labour' controlling Scottish Labour. Meanwhile, the SNP was seen as having operated as a 'loyal opposition' in Holyrood, consciously projecting an image of respectability while maintaining the party's reputation for standing up to London when necessary.

On the 'domestic' front, the question was simply whether the SNP could offer capable and decisive government. With opposition parties, especially those with no previous record in office, assessing likely performance is difficult (Butt, 2006). But there are grounds for educated guesswork: did the party seem united and competent in opposition? Do its promises seem credible? Does its leader seem up to the job? The repetition of 'seem' in these questions emphasises that this is a matter of voters' impressions or image of the party. And the SNP put a good deal of effort into managing its 'brand' as the 2007 elections approached. The motivating force was Martin Seligman's (1998) argument that optimism beats pessimism at the ballot box. This inspired a conscious effort to accentuate the positive in campaigning. Since Labour, seeking to eat into their opponent's poll lead, focused closely on the risks of an SNP victory, the campaign became an unusually clear-cut contest between positive and negative messages – and, as such, in some ways provided a foretaste of the 2014 referendum campaign. There is no simple answer to the question of whether hope or fear is a more powerful electoral weapon (see Lau et al., 2007, for a comprehensive assessment). It depends on how skilfully each is wielded, on which voters are targeted, and on where a party needs to strengthen its hand. In the case of the SNP, at that time yet to make the transition 'from protest to power', it is not hard to see why emphasising a positive agenda for government would prove more resonant than criticising from the sidelines. And there is clear evidence that the

SNP's positive approach in 2007 was not only noticed by voters but paid electoral dividends (Pattie et al., 2011).

Alex Salmond's image also received a makeover. In preparation for the 2007 campaign, advisers gave him training in how to come across as a more statesmanlike and rather less combative figure than before. We stressed the electoral importance of leadership in the previous chapter; that importance is redoubled in cases like this, where the party is untested in office but the leader has been long established in his position. Even though Salmond had never been First Minister, his thirteen years over two stints as party leader gave clear indications about his likely style and performance in the top job. Insofar as there was respect – grudging or otherwise – for his competence and authority, this will not only have generated a personal vote but also have shaped expectations of an SNP government under his leadership. At the same time, the platform that Holyrood had given to other senior SNP figures helped to counter accusations that the party was a 'one-man band'. Nicola Sturgeon in particular had performed well in Holyrood, especially when standing in at First Minister's Questions, and had become a well-known figure in Scottish politics. This made it easier for voters to imagine the SNP as a governing team (even if one with a very assertive captain). Indeed, the use of 'Alex Salmond for First Minister' on the regional list ballot was aimed not only at capitalising on this leadership asset but also at emphasising that the SNP could be a governing party.

Seeking to explain the unprecedented SNP success in the general election of October 1974, William Miller suggested that:

> ... the purely party, as distinct from policy, characteristics of the SNP were far from repulsive. While the party might never have been able to take up a large measure of its natural support without the help of conditions such as those in 1974 which predisposed people throughout Britain towards deserting the old governing parties, the SNP had the image, the organisation, and the enthusiasm to take the opportunity... (1981: 258–9)

Something very similar might be said of the 2007 election. Plenty of Scottish voters were predisposed to desert the governing Labour Party (or had done so already), and the SNP had the image, organisation and enthusiasm to take advantage. However, not everyone was convinced. Thirty-three per cent of constituency votes and 31 per cent of regional list votes represented the SNP's best ever electoral performance but it was only just enough to emerge as the largest party and it meant that more than two thirds of Scottish voters had rejected the party's offer. Many of these will have been diehard Unionists, never in the SNP's reach. Many others, though, will have given the party some consideration before deciding to look elsewhere on the ballot. There remained doubts about the SNP's general readiness to govern, fears about placing Scotland's economy and public services in the hands of novices, and suspicions that the SNP might be more hell-bent on independence than its campaign tone implied. Over the next four years, it became clear that winning those voters round was a high priority for Salmond and his party.

MINORITY RULE

The 2007 result could hardly have been closer. The SNP had won forty-seven and Labour forty-six seats. Yet the SNP's narrow victory was not the first shock of election night. The final result of the election only became known nineteen hours after polls had closed, when the list results were finally announced for the Highlands and Islands. The count across Scotland had been marred by a remarkably large proportion of spoiled ballot papers. Subsequent research and an official inquiry concluded that this had been caused by the poor design of the ballot paper, which had confused some of the electorate (Carman et al., 2008; Gould, 2007). Then there was a miscalculation in the allocation of Highland list seats such that the overall result was very nearly declared for Labour. This error by the Highland Council staff was only noticed at the last minute by Dave Thompson, SNP list candidate and a former senior council official. The mistake would, no doubt, eventually have been realised and corrected but it would have cast a shadow over the election outcome and thus over the SNP's first chance to hold executive power.

Indeed, given that the controversies over ballot design and counting at this election generated at least a passing resemblance with Florida at the 2000 US presidential election, it was doubly crucial for the legitimacy of the new government that the administrative problems and the election results were seen largely as independent of one another.

A despondent Labour was slow to respond to the result while the SNP immediately declared itself the winner. Alex Salmond flew into Edinburgh by helicopter and, drawing on the statesmanship training mentioned above, made a speech in the grounds of Prestonfield House Hotel. 'It is very clear indeed', he insisted, 'which party has lost this election, and the Labour Party no longer has any moral authority left to govern Scotland.' There was nothing to prevent a combination of parties with an overall majority from forming a government. But the Liberal Democrats with sixteen seats had declared that they would no longer work in coalition with Labour; and the Conservatives with seventeen had maintained all along that they would not join any other party – not that they had an obvious partner in any case – but would instead adopt a position of constructive opposition to whichever party was in minority government, supporting it in the annual Budget and other key votes. Labour's general dejection and lack of plausible coalition options, combined with the SNP's largest-party status and consequent projection of itself as the winner, created obvious momentum leading up to the vote in Holyrood for the election of Scotland's First Minister.

The SNP made overtures to the Liberal Democrats but were rejected and instead reached a loose 'cooperation agreement' with the Greens. The additional two MSPs made little difference but contributed to an impression of the SNP being open to ideas and willing to work with other parties. The more significant relationships to develop, however, were outside Parliament. SNP ministers forged good working relations with a range of bodies and interests, building on contacts developed while in opposition. A concordat was signed with the Convention of Scottish Local Authorities (CoSLA) to remove many of the detailed controls about which local government had long complained and to guarantee local government funding through to the end of the parliament. Having fought the election on a promise to freeze council tax, the SNP then offered Scotland's local authorities compensating funding. This brought about improved relations between central and local government, thus removing a potential source of tension over the four years ahead.

On his election as First Minister, Alex Salmond acknowledged that the absence of an overall majority required a different style of politics. The new parliament would be 'about compromise and concession, intelligent debate and mature discussion' and he intended to 'reach across the parties and try to build a majority, issue by issue' (Scottish Parliament, 16 May 2007). This carried an echo of the talk a decade before, in the lead-up to the establishment of the Scottish Parliament, when there was a naïve belief in some quarters that an electoral system which made single-party majority government unlikely would lead to a 'new politics' of consensus and compromise. When Salmond asserted that the SNP would govern according to devolution's founding principles, then, there was some basis to this but he was making a virtue of necessity. While hoping to govern in coalition, the party had also prepared for minority government and studied its operation elsewhere.

Nonetheless, most commentators in May 2007 expected that the SNP would not last the full four-year term. It had never been in power before, and minority government tended to be associated with instability. Key to the administration's survival would be relations with the other parties and the need to build majorities issue by issue. This might require 'patchwork agreements' whereby 'different combinations of parties support different elements' of measures, including Budgets and legislation (Green-Pedersen, 2001, p. 63). Bruce Crawford became Minister for Parliamentary Business and took responsibility for negotiations with other parties. If judged by the government's ability to avoid embarrassing defeats, he was very successful in this role. There was only one occasion on which the SNP was unexpectedly defeated on a key vote – and that was reversed within days. In 2009, the two Green MSPs voted with Labour and Liberal Democrat MSPs against the Budget. The resulting tie forced the Presiding Officer, Alex Fergusson, into a casting vote which he used controversially to vote down the Budget and potentially to precipitate an election. However, with polls suggesting that the SNP would be returned with a clearer lead over its rivals, neither Labour nor the Liberal Democrats wanted another election, and a slightly revised Budget was passed within a week, with only the Greens voting against. The episode ended up backfiring on the opposition parties, giving the impression that the SNP was trying its best to govern in difficult circumstances while Labour was simply being oppositional.

But it was not only the absence of a parliamentary majority that tested this SNP administration. Within its first year in power, the global financial crisis created a series of painful headaches for the Scottish government. Although macroeconomic matters were retained at Westminster, the financial shock would have adverse economic, fiscal and political consequences for the SNP, challenging the optimistic message that the party had sought to make its leitmotiv. In particular, the remarkable success of the Royal Bank of Scotland (RBS) had been much praised by the party and especially its leader. Salmond, who had worked as an economist for the bank before becoming an MP, had gone so far in 2007 as to laud it as the 'pride of the "Celtic Lion"' economy that he envisaged would match what had been happening across the Irish Sea. There was a broader belief in party circles that RBS's success had contributed to a more positive Scottish brand. The upshot was that the bank's near-collapse had the potential not only of tarnishing that brand but also of undermining the SNP in the process. However, the party sustained relatively little damage since Salmond and the SNP were far from alone in having basked in the reflected glory of RBS's rise, and since ultimately the public did not see responsibility for the financial turmoil as lying with the Scottish government.

Devolved public spending had risen by an annual average of 5 per cent in real terms in the years before the SNP came to power. These were the most dramatic increases in expenditure across the UK during any period outside wartime. With the financial crisis, this would come to an abrupt end, and governments across the UK faced a reversal of that trend. The SNP had therefore come to power at the start of the most difficult point for public spending. It was clear from the start that the party was over, to borrow the term used by Labour minister Tony Crosland when facing an earlier financial crisis in 1975. However, they benefited from two mitigating circumstances. The first was the Conservative promise in the run-up to the 2010 UK general election to protect Scotland's spending in its first year in power. This was part of the Tories' 'respect agenda', designed to address its image problem in Scotland. The second, echoing the point about RBS above, is that it was to the Westminster government that most Scottish voters continued to ascribe fiscal responsibility – and blame. As described in the next section, the incumbent SNP became regarded as Scotland's defenders against the cuts.

As a minority government, the SNP was also able to save face in abandoning manifesto commitments that had had popular appeal but would prove difficult to implement.

Its commitment to a local income tax (LIT) dated back many decades but would have involved a radical overhaul of local government finance. Governments attempt such reforms at their peril. The Liberal Democrats, also committed to the introduction of LIT, were just as keen to avoid becoming entangled in a complex reform that would create losers as well as winners and would have required much time and effort over the course of the parliament. Similarly, the SNP quietly dropped a commitment to a first-time buyers' grant of £2,000, a policy thought by some housing specialists unlikely to have any impact beyond inflating house prices (Lloyd, 2007). The party was able to shelve the plan following a public consultation. It succeeded in winning cross-party support for a number of popular measures. Tolls across the Forth and Tay road bridges were abolished and the graduate endowment paid by students after graduation was scrapped. The SNP also followed Labour in Wales in introducing free NHS prescriptions. In terms of policy, then, the SNP avoided major and potentially contentious reforms, aiming to build voters' trust in the party as a safe option for government while offering some popular measures. Crucially, the SNP gained a general reputation for competence against a much more challenging backdrop than had previously existed.

Perhaps the most notable departure from that approach, and the most controversial move made by the SNP government in its first term in office, was Justice Secretary Kenny MacAskill's decision to release the only man convicted of the

1988 Lockerbie bombing, Abdelbaset al-Megrahi, on compassionate grounds as he was suffering from terminal cancer. The reaction from the SNP's opponents was swift and caught the government off guard. They had anticipated opposition but were unprepared for the vehemence of the attacks from the UK government, especially given that London had been negotiating the release of Megrahi with the Libyan government for some time. American embassy officials' reports on the situation, later to surface among the vast collection of papers available through Wikileaks, noted that the 'UK government has gotten everything – a chance to stick it to Salmond's Scottish National Party (SNP) and good relations with Libya' while Scotland got 'nothing' (*Guardian*, 2010). In contrast to the widespread condemnation of the decision in the US, and to a lesser extent that in the rest of the UK, public opinion in Scotland was rather more mixed, and softened over time towards MacAskill's decision. Nonetheless, there was a period immediately after the announcement when the SNP government's position looked more precarious than at any other time during its four years in office. And the experience probably reinforced the leadership's determination to pursue a 'safety first' strategy.

The big problem with that strategy was that it sat uneasily with the party's commitment to independence. The leadership was well aware that the party's core support and activists would expect to see at least some progress on that front. It therefore engaged in symbolic politics. Within days of the election, workmen were seen changing the large letters above

the entrance to Victoria Quay, headquarters of what had
been the 'Scottish executive' and from then on would be called
the 'Scottish government'. This renaming had been originally
proposed by Henry McLeish, then Labour First Minister,
in 2001 but was opposed by his colleagues in government in
London. The decision to go ahead with the name change was a
symbol of the new government's desire to be more independent.
But the impetus for the change had, in fact, come from senior
civil servants rather than the SNP, with some in the party's
leadership fearing that it might be seen as a provocative move.

More significantly, the SNP government embarked on
what it called a 'national conversation' when it launched
the White Paper on 'Choosing Scotland's Future' in August
2007 (Scottish Executive, 2007). As described in the following chapter, the document was remarkable not only because
it was the first official document that made the case for
Scottish independence but also because of the prominent role
it allowed to devolution – that word appeared more times
than the word 'independence'. The notion that the SNP would
have produced such a document would have been unthinkable a generation before. Kenny MacAskill personified this
shift. He had been a hardline fundamentalist in the 1980s
and early 1990s but by 2004 was arguing for a longer-term
strategy via the strengthening of the Scottish Parliament – or,
as he put it, 'not living the dream but improving the reality'
(MacAskill, 2004). While not all of the party's senior figures took such a gradualist position, the SNP leadership as

a whole could be said essentially to have put independence on the backburner, and was able to claim that the lack of an overall majority prevented it doing otherwise.

But the question then arose of how the party could use its position in office to further the cause of independence. So long as it retained popular support, the SNP appeared to subscribe to the argument that governing competently would lead to increased support for independence. The problem was that the evidence – as shown in Figure 5.1 – suggested otherwise. While support for the party was strengthening, support for independence remained resolutely unchanged. The issue was whether – or, perhaps more likely, *when* – the activists would become impatient and start asking whether ministerial office was benefiting a few members but doing nothing to bring about the change desired. Had the SNP won another term of minority government in 2011, that question would probably have become more and more pertinent. In the event, however, the party's unexpected majority changed the picture entirely.

AN UNEXPECTED MAJORITY

In 2007, the SNP had won only narrowly because, despite scoring well on 'the image, the organisation and the enthusiasm', as highlighted earlier, there were fears about how an SNP-led government would perform in Scotland and behave within the Union. In 2011, the party won handsomely because it retained those previous advantages and, after a term in office, had allayed voters' fears – particularly about an SNP government immediately bundling Scotland into a van marked 'Independence'.

In fact, the party looked to have done more than simply ease the voters' worst fears; it had positively impressed them. No election outcome can be explained in a single statistic but, in the case of 2011, the +36 in the bottom left of Table 5.1 goes a long way. Fifty-six per cent of respondents – almost twice the proportion that had voted for the SNP four years earlier – felt that the party's performance in office had been fairly good or very good, compared to just 20 per cent delivering a negative verdict. This not only provides the sole net positive rating of any party in the table but is startlingly positive. Voters are generally lavish in their criticism and miserly in their praise. So, while the gap between the ratings of the SNP's actual and Labour's hypothetical performance is easily wide enough to explain the big SNP victory, there is nothing ruinous in the Labour figures. It is the SNP rating that stands out. Approval for the SNP at Holyrood even outstrips *dis*approval of the Conservatives at Westminster – an impressive feat in the Scottish context. In sum, if oppositions have to wait for incumbents to lose elections, then Labour had no chance in 2011.

Why, then, was the SNP government evaluated so positively? The party's supporters might reject the querulous tone in that question, regarding these ratings instead as credit where credit was due. And, in the absence of agreed and

TABLE 5.1: EVALUATIONS OF GOVERNING PARTY PERFORMANCE
AT HOLYROOD AND WESTMINSTER

HOW GOOD A JOB DONE BY...

| | AT HOLYROOD | | AT WESTMINSTER | | |
| | SNP 2007–2011 | LABOUR *IF* IN POWER | LABOUR 1997–2010 | CON 2010– | LIB DEM 2010– |
	%	%	%	%	%
Very good	14	4	5	4	1
Fairly good	42	27	31	18	13
Neither	25	26	19	23	23
Fairly bad	12	25	21	25	26
Very bad	8	18	25	30	36
Good – Bad	**+36**	**-12**	**-10**	**-33**	**-48**
N	*1,923*	*1,613*	*1,967*	*1,951*	*1,943*

Source: Scottish Election Study, 2011

objective measures of government performance, we cannot simply declare these perceptions to be mistaken. Yet we
would sum up the previous section as describing a broadly
satisfactory term of office rather than a catalogue of successes. Moreover, when asked in additional survey questions
about outcomes in the key devolved areas of health, education and law and order, on balance voters felt that standards
were falling rather than rising. So that +36 rating still looks
surprisingly high. One possibility is that voters see governing by any party as a matter of disaster-aversion – especially
in an economically challenging context. On that reading,
the absence of obvious failure is in itself a success. Or perhaps minority governments are given an easier ride in these

assessments, being forgiven for any failure to meet their manifesto commitments while rewarded where they do deliver on
their manifesto, as for example with the council tax freeze.
Combine that with the perception that the SNP government
had stood up for Scotland, especially in the context of the
return of a Conservative-led government in London, and
the party had a winning formula.

We place most weight on a third possibility, though, which
might be called the 'panic over' explanation. According to the
party's opponents, an SNP administration was supposed to
usher in a period of conflict and turmoil as the party pursued
independence, even if initially only in the form of a referendum. As Labour activist Ian Smart vividly put it, his party's
campaigning had been 'premised on the election of an SNP
government leading to a flight of capital, the collapse of the
Scottish economy, schools and hospitals closing their doors
out of a sheer sense of hopelessness and ultimately plagues of
locusts ravaging the land' (cited in Hassan and Shaw, 2012,
p. 144). On polling day in 2007, the Scottish edition of *The
Sun*'s front cover showed a picture of a hangman's noose
with the warning 'Vote SNP today and you put Scotland's
head in the noose'. Insofar as voters expected anything like
that, on top of quite reasonable fears about a party as yet
untested in office, they will have been pleasantly surprised by
what happened. A relieved 'actually, they were pretty good'
verdict was the upshot – including from the Scottish *Sun*,
which by 2011 was endorsing the SNP.

Admittedly, this 'panic over' thesis might sound trite compared to an explanation based on data about voters' evaluations of policies and their outcomes. Yet in fact it better describes what we know about citizens' political judgements more generally, which is that they are simple rather than complex – a broad impression rather than a detailed assessment of a government's record – and that they are often driven by emotional reactions like anger or fear as much as dispassionate calculation. (In the jargon of political psychology, they are affective rather than simply cognitive.) It may well be that a kind of accountant's balance sheet, carefully recording the 2007–11 government's successes and failures, would have delivered a different verdict. But voters do not compile detailed balance sheets, either literally or figuratively. Instead, they rely on general impressions of a party, and their overriding judgement is based on the question that evolution has trained us to ask: Do I need to worry about this lot or not? (Marcus et al., 2000, provide a much more sophisticated account of the role of anxiety in voting behaviour.)

Having persuaded many voters that they need not worry about turmoil in the pursuit of independence, the SNP government could then capitalise fully on its other advantages. These were as in 2007 – only more so. Alex Salmond's personal likeability rating had improved compared with the last election, giving him a big advantage over Jack McConnell's replacement (via Wendy Alexander) as Labour leader, Iain Gray. And there is no clearer indicator of grudging respect

than the fact that, even among self-professed Labour supporters who watched the TV debates, 64 per cent declared
Salmond to have been the strongest performer. Meanwhile,
the party's quest to be seen as campaigning positively was a
resounding success. Seventy-one per cent of Scottish Election
Study respondents described the SNP's campaign as 'very' or
'fairly positive', up from 51 per cent in 2007. As with the
performance evaluations above, these are much larger proportions than ended up voting for the party and so there is at
least some objective component to these assessments – they
are not just a meaningless case of voters simply declaring
'their team' to be positive and everyone else to be negative.
It was therefore also bad news for Labour that nearly two
in three voters (63 per cent) assessed their campaign as negative, reflecting the perceived contrast in approach between
the leading contenders for office. The SNP's determinedly
positive approach is more noteworthy given that, well into
2011, polls were suggesting a Labour win. Even as speculation in the press mounted and Labour grew more confident
of a return to power at Holyrood, the SNP kept its nerve.
There were few voices demanding a change of leader or a
change of strategy.

Perhaps voters liked the SNP because of this positivity;
maybe they perceived positive messages because they already
liked the look of the party. What is clear is that in 2011 the
SNP projected an image that was favourable more or less
across the board. Table 5.2 shows, first for the two leading

contenders in 2011, the percentages of voters who deemed
each description to apply to the party in question. Considered
in isolation, the Labour scores do not look bad. Aside from
'keeping promises', which voters think happens so rarely that
they do not even expect it of parties anyway (see Naurin,
2011), Scottish Labour got the thumbs-up from more than
half of the electorate on each of the other four criteria. Yet it
trailed the SNP, often by some distance, on all five, because the
latter's scores were so high. We get a clearer picture of how
high by comparing with two other recent winning parties, this
time from Westminster elections (and based on ratings from
the British electorate as a whole). The SNP in 2011 was seen
as clearly more united, more in touch and more trustworthy
than either Labour in 2001 or Conservatives in 2010 (both
of which won healthy shares, 41 per cent and 37 per cent

TABLE 5.2: PARTIES' RATINGS ON FIVE FACETS OF PARTY IMAGE

% OF RESPONDENTS AGREEING THAT THAT PARTY IS...	SCOTTISH SAMPLE ONLY		ALL BRITISH RESPONDENTS	
	SNP 2011	LAB 2011	LAB 2001	CON 2010
United	86	52	70	61
In touch with ordinary people	75	57	54	36
Keep their promises	50	31	43	34
Capable of strong government	71	62	84	71
Standing up for Scotland	95	56	—	—

Sources: Scottish Election Study, 2011; British Election Studies, 2001, 2010

respectively, of the British vote). Only on capacity for strong government does the SNP come in second, and then only to the impressive 84 per cent scored by Tony Blair's Labour.

Two of the 2011 comparisons in that table are worth highlighting, given their role in the SNP's supplanting of Labour as Scotland's dominant party. First, there is the SNP's noticeable advantage on being 'in touch with ordinary people'. This represents the same kind of incursion into traditional Labour territory as was seen on election night in 2011 when, from the gains in East Kilbride and Hamilton onwards, the story was one of the SNP sweeping into Labour's erstwhile west of Scotland strongholds. In Chapter 8, we look in more detail at the changing profile of the SNP's electorate. Suffice it to say here that there is an obvious link between the party being credited for concern about ordinary people and its capacity to win seats in Scotland's most deprived areas.

If being in touch with ordinary people was one of Labour's *raisons d'être*, then 'standing up for Scotland' has always been one of the SNP's – indeed, 'the furtherance of all Scottish interests' is given equal billing alongside independence in the party's constitution. Going back to the party's 1974 breakthroughs, William Miller found that the 'overwhelming majority of Scottish electors [including three-quarters of Labour and Conservative voters] felt the SNP's existence and electoral successes had been "good for Scotland"' (1981, p. 92). No surprise, then, that the party leads the way in Figure 5.2. This graph shows the percentage of respondents rating each party in either of the top two of four categories (i.e. on the credit side of the ledger) on the question of how far they can be trusted to look after Scotland's interests. Perhaps more surprising is that, if the gap between the SNP and Labour on this criterion has never been wider than in 2011, this is not because of any continuing deterioration of Labour's rating. They have held steady since devolution and so the SNP's widening advantage is owed to their own improved ratings on 'Scotland's interests'.

FIGURE 5.2: SNP, LABOUR AND CONSERVATIVE RATINGS
ON 'LOOKING AFTER SCOTLAND'S INTERESTS'

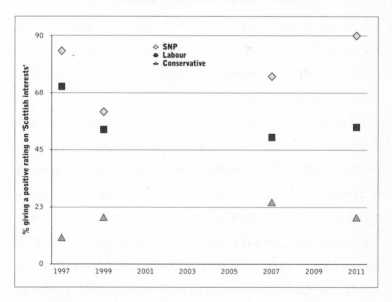

Note: The wording of the question changed between 1999 and 2007, with a scale from 'Just about always' to 'Almost never' being replaced by one from 'Very closely' to 'Not at all closely'.

Sources: Scottish Election Survey, 1997; Scottish Social Attitudes Survey, 1999; Scottish Election Studies, 2007 and 2011.

This rather belies any narrative about secular Labour decline in this regard. If equivalent data were available from the 1980s and early 1990s, they might reveal that period as a high-water mark for Labour on standing up for Scotland against the Conservative government. But those final four words are crucial here. As Figure 5.2 confirms for the past twenty years – and as was doubtless also true for the twenty before that – Labour has had no problem in far outstripping the Conservatives on 'Scottish interests'. And in Westminster elections, at least until 2015, that was the comparison that mattered – and the SNP's even higher rating was not very relevant. What changed with devolution, then, was not the ranking of the parties but the relevant comparison. In Scottish Parliament elections, Labour's longstanding advantage over the Conservatives is less relevant than their longstanding deficit with respect to the SNP.

That deficit was at its narrowest in 1999. We mentioned earlier that there is no hard and fast rule when it comes to campaigning – going negative can work but can backfire – and one explanation for the SNP dip on Scottish interests is that Labour managed to portray the SNP's policies as damaging to Scotland. Independence was one target, of course, but Labour was also heavily critical of more specific SNP plans such as using Holyrood's tax-varying powers to add a 'penny for Scotland' on income tax. Murray Ritchie's (2000) account of the election points to a concerted and no-holds-barred Labour campaign to erode voters' trust in the SNP as defenders of Scottish interests. Labour cautioned that the untested SNP would push hard for independence. Its first election poster in 1999 warned anyone tempted to give the SNP a chance: 'Divorce is an expensive business. It won't be a trial separation with the SNP.'

If this was successful, it wasn't quite successful enough. Labour still trailed slightly on the Scottish interests criterion – and this mattered electorally. Lindsay Paterson and colleagues showed that doubts about Labour in this regard predicted defection from the party in 1999: they concluded that 'the principal reason for Labour's "under-performance" in the first Scottish election was that it was not thought sufficiently capable of standing up for Scotland's interests within the Union' (2001, p. 41). And this remained a problem in subsequent Holyrood contests, exacerbated by Labour's increasingly obdurate stance against further devolution. Even voters who themselves prefer the status quo tend to regard a party's openness to 'more powers' as a signal of its commitment to stand up for Scotland (Johns et al., 2010, pp. 119–20).

That leaves the question of why the SNP's credentials have improved since 1999. This may partly be explained by the general burnishing of the party's image. If the SNP is thought more competent, more united, better led and so on, then it is presumably also better equipped to work in Scotland's interests and to deliver on manifesto commitments in difficult circumstances. However, devolution played a key enabling role here. We noted in Chapter 3 that more SNP parliamentarians were returned in the first election to Holyrood than had ever previously been elected to the House of Commons. This brought additional resources and, crucially, greater media attention to the party – especially as the Scottish media began to focus more on events in Edinburgh than at Westminster. As first a potential and then an actual Scottish government, the SNP could stand up for Scottish interests in governing practice rather than simply in rhetoric from the Westminster sidelines. Judging by the graph, voters in 2007 seemed confident in the party's willingness to do this and, by 2011, clearly felt that that optimism had not been misplaced.

If devolution is indeed crucial here, then there is no contradiction between the widening SNP–Labour gap in Figure 5.2 and the strong Labour showing in the 2010 general election. In that Westminster contest, Labour was by far the best of the *viable* options to fight for Scottish interests. While lacking the data to continue the graph to 2015, we are confident that the bigger shift was not in the ratings of the parties but in the *relevance* of the SNP's rating at that election. Meanwhile, when it comes to Scottish elections, the SNP has long been established as the option most trusted to work in Scotland's interests.

Of course, 'standing up for Scottish interests' is a very vague notion. But that does not make it unimportant electorally. We mentioned earlier that voters are rarely much interested in or informed about the details of policy, instead forming broad impressions of the parties among which they must choose at election time. Perceptions of the priority that a party gives to Scotland's interests within the Union are exactly the kind of impressions that could make up a floating voter's mind for or against that party.

In 2011, however, there was a specific arena in which aspiring Holyrood governments were pledging to stand up for Scottish interests. Both the SNP and Labour sought explicitly to present themselves as Scotland's best defence against the expenditure-cutting agenda of the Westminster coalition. As with Scottish interests in general, Labour again won some credit in this regard, with 48 per cent of Scottish Election Study respondents judging the party likely to be either 'very' or 'fairly' effective at managing the impact of spending cuts. Again, however, Labour trailed the SNP, for whom the corresponding figure was 64 per cent. Having made this issue central to its campaigning in 2011, Scottish Labour were fighting on terrain that better suited its main rival. Voters are likelier to remember the name of the sandwich chain in which Iain Gray sought refuge than to remember that he had been pursued in there by a group called 'Citizens United Against Cuts to Public Services', fronted by veteran socialist protestor Sean Clerkin. (Clerkin pursued other party leaders, including Annabel Goldie from the Conservatives, but Labour were the ones seen as running away.) This further illustrates Labour's failure to establish itself as Scotland's leading anti-austerity party – more ground instead occupied by the SNP.

Given all this voter enthusiasm, the SNP's majority in 2011 might look anything but accidental. Yet, even if constitutional fears had been eased by the party's approach in government, the strong popular majority against independence was expected to remain a brake on the SNP's electoral support. And it was Labour who led in the polls for most of the year between their strong general election showing and the Holyrood contest in 2011. Not until early April, only four weeks before polling day, did any opinion poll show an SNP lead on the regional list vote. Indeed, throughout the entire campaign, not a single poll showed an SNP regional vote as high as the 44 per cent that the party received, and only one poll – the very final one – showed a Labour regional vote as low as their eventual 26 per cent.

Had the polls foreshadowed the final SNP vote share, attention might then have turned – not just among constitutional anoraks but also among the media and the campaigning parties – to the not-quite-so-proportional workings of the Scottish electoral system. The one thing that everyone (thought they) knew about the Scottish Parliament's mixed-member system was that it was proportional so as to make it very difficult for the SNP to win a majority and then to impose independence. In the end, as mentioned in Chapter 3, the system wasn't proportional enough to make it difficult enough in 2011. There was a recipe for a majority based on a vote share in the mid-40s. By sweeping the constituency board in its strongholds (like northeast Scotland) while doing well enough in other regions (like the south of Scotland) to earn some list seats, the SNP won 53.5 per cent of the seats – which, given the levels of party unity on show during its 2007–11 term, was very much a working majority.

Before moving on from the 2011 election, we should return to the point made clearly at the outset of this chapter. The SNP's major gains were made in spite of, not because of, the party's flagship constitutional policy. Support for independence between 2007 and 2011 remained stable and at a much lower percentage than the SNP's eventual support. Victory was achieved, then, by winning over large numbers of voters who remained opposed to independence. Key to this were voters' favourable reports on the SNP's performance in government and favourable impressions of its leader, its trustworthiness and its commitment to Scottish interests within the Union. However, no less important were the promise of a referendum and a general strategy of downplaying the constitutional question in favour of emphasising governing competence. In other words, the SNP was seen as a safe pair of hands partly because, via its apparent moderation and commitment to a referendum, Scotland was kept safely in the Union. The irony at the heart of the 2011 Scottish election, then, is that it was exactly the SNP's easing of fears on the independence question that brought them the votes that might ultimately deliver it.

THE LUXURY OF A MAJORITY?

Our aim in this chapter has not been to form an objective assessment of whether the SNP truly was a safe pair of hands in office. That is not only a very difficult task but also, for

present purposes, an irrelevant one. We are interested in
what the voters thought. Of course SNP diehards will have
thought its governing record more or less impeccable, while
its detractors will have seen only catastrophe. More impor-
tantly, the average Scottish voter will have been, on balance,
impressed. All three views are merely perceptions. And, like
all perceptions, they are coloured by expectations. Some will
say that the SNP's positive evaluations are because expectations were so low, or fears were so high, that mere disaster
aversion would be enough to reassure voters. (If those fears
were exaggerated by the SNP's opponents, there is further
irony in the party profiting from such lowered expectations.)
Others might suggest that voters' expectations of *all* governments are quite limited and that, like referees in football, the
good governments are the ones that you don't notice. In that
case, the fact that the SNP's terms of office have been relatively uneventful is enough to win them approval. In any
event, the important point is that the SNP were somewhat
successful in 2007 and very successful in 2011 at presenting
themselves to the electorate as an unthreatening, indeed an
attractive, proposition.

Of course, having won its surprise majority, the SNP
immediately became a much more threatening proposition
to the clear majority opposed to independence. As surprised
as anyone by the outcome, the party's leadership needed to
find a new way of reconciling the SNP's constitutional ambitions with the recipe for electoral success described in this

chapter. This was a tricky balance to strike because, as we will see, electoral success had become for that leadership – though not for many of its activists – rather more than merely a means to the end of independence.

Clearly, the question of independence and a referendum could no longer simply be parked. Initially, there were questions about whether it was constitutional for the Scottish Parliament to legislate for a referendum on independence, given that the constitution was a retained matter under the terms of the devolution legislation. This meant that the first vote in the new Holyrood parliamentary term, the election of Presiding Officer, took on great significance, given that he or she would have to rule on whether proposed legislation was *intra vires*. It therefore proved controversial when Tricia Marwick of the SNP was elected with the backing of the party's new majority. In the event, the UK government agreed to devolve the power to hold a referendum. Negotiations between the two governments about the rules and procedures for conducting the referendum resulted in the Edinburgh Agreement.

Governing in the run-up to the referendum carried on largely as before. The SNP were keen to avoid controversies that might undermine support for independence and so pursued the same 'safety first' approach as in their first term of office. While there were many detailed commitments in the manifesto, the emphasis was on continuity and the defence of Scottish interests, summed up in the workmanlike slogan

'Re-elect a Scottish government working for Scotland'. Given the chilly economic and fiscal climate, and in the absence of borrowing powers for the Scottish government, balancing the Budget remained the biggest challenge. This needed to be squared with meeting the 2011 election promises of a council tax freeze, no compulsory redundancies in the public sector, creating a single fire and rescue service and reducing the number of police forces while still employing one thousand more police officers.

If there is not that much more to say about the SNP's second term of office, that is a measure of just how far Scottish politics became dominated by the referendum. The party's unchanging approach to everyday government suggested that its 'safe pair of hands' strategy for fighting Holyrood elections would be pursued next time around, too. However, if the seismic impact of the referendum on the UK general election in 2015 is anything to go by, 2016 will depend on more than simply which party seems best to govern Scotland under the existing arrangements. In the upcoming chapters, we look at the referendum and its reshaping of electoral choice in Scotland. One key question, always keeping one eye on this chapter, is whether the SNP can ride that radical wave of support for independence while maintaining the image of solidity and respectability that won the party its breakthroughs in Holyrood.

Meanwhile, it is worth ending with a word about Labour, given their prominent supporting role in this chapter. Plenty has been written about the decline of Scottish Labour (which, at the time of writing, appeared to be an ongoing process) and, since this is a book about the SNP, our remit is not to contribute to that. In fact, one of the striking features of the survey data reported in this chapter is that Labour's ratings have often continued to be quite respectable. Assessed in *absolute* terms, the party was not seen as incompetent, out of touch or anti-Scottish. Labour's problem was that elections are fought in *relative* terms. So the party lost in 2007 and 2011 because it was seen as less competent, less in touch with ordinary people and less ready to fight for Scotland's interests than the SNP. The danger for Labour is that the distinction between relative and absolute can become blurred because voting is inherently a comparative exercise. If a narrative develops whereby the Labour Party is portrayed as anti-Scottish relative to its chief rival, Labour and anti-Scottishness may become associated in voters' minds. For many years, of course, the party benefited from exactly this process. In those years the Conservatives were seen as anti-Scottish, and Labour much less so, and so Labour were viewed as the ones standing up for Scotland. But devolution brought about a new focus of comparison, and with it a weakening of Labour's reputation and a slump in its electoral fortunes. Indeed, if the SNP and Labour are occupying the same ideological territory but the former has an in-built advantage when it comes to being seen to fight for Scottish interests, the SNP may eventually supplant Labour and render it irrelevant.

CHAPTER 6
THE LONG ROAD TO 2014

O ne common criticism of political parties, especially after they suffer electoral defeats, is that 'it was not clear what they stood for'. This has never been the case for the SNP. It has always been clear where the party wants to go. How to get there, how quickly to get there and in particular whether to get there via devolution – these are the controversies that run deepest in the SNP. In this chapter, we chart the party's pursuit of constitutional change over the past forty years or more, examining how these longstanding tensions played out. The chapter ends on the crowning irony

that it was the almost total dominance of pragmatism that
eventually brought Scotland to the brink of independence.

FUNDAMENTALISTS AND GRADUALISTS

A challenge that many of the SNP's opponents have in understanding the party is that the familiar left/right or liberal/
conservative divisions are neither the only, nor even the most
important, tensions inside the SNP. Given the largely class-
based nature of the Scottish party system prior to the SNP's
advance, the emergence of a party that focused on a territorial
or 'centre-periphery' cleavage proved difficult to grasp. Labour
described the SNP as 'tartan Tories' and the Tories described
them as 'tartan socialists'. For much of its history, the SNP lived
in fear of being seen as too close to one or other of the two
main parties. In the 1970s, it kept a record of its MPs' votes
in Parliament to demonstrate its relative even-handedness in
supporting and opposing the Labour government.

When the SNP became a serious electoral threat, its
opponents offered weak measures of devolution. This created problems for the party. Should it support a measure of
devolution on the grounds that this was a step towards its
ultimate goal, or oppose it on the grounds that the motivation behind such offers was to undermine the SNP and stop
any move towards independence in its tracks? The Tories
were first to offer a measure of home rule when Ted Heath

made his 'Declaration of Perth' in 1968, but it was Labour's promise in 1974 to deliver a directly elected assembly that issued the main challenge. Events in the 1970s may seem distant now but would cast a shadow over the SNP and have an impact on internal SNP politics for a generation. No attempt to understand the SNP pre-devolution is possible without an appreciation of the impact of the late 1970s on the party.

The Tories had failed to implement plans to establish a Scottish assembly on coming to power in 1970 and so the SNP doubted the Tories' renewed commitment in the two elections in 1974. But the SNP thought its electoral rise meant that Labour was more likely to keep its commitment to a directly elected assembly as set out in Labour's manifesto in October 1974. A year later, in November 1975, the Wilson government brought forward its White Paper, 'Our Changing Democracy'. The following May, the SNP debated its response at its annual conference in Motherwell. The decision was that the party should reaffirm its commitment to independence 'though prepared to accept an assembly with limited powers as a possible stepping stone'. An attempt to remove this caveat was defeated but 40 per cent of delegates had supported its deletion. Thereafter, however, the party largely united around supporting devolution.

But Labour was deeply divided on devolution and, having won an overall majority of only four seats in October 1974, the government was vulnerable to backbench rebellions. With some sceptics even among the Liberals, the SNP

and Plaid Cymru were the only parties united in support
of the Scotland & Wales Bill, the Labour government's first
devolution bill that was brought before the Commons in
late 1976. The following February, after very slow progress
as opponents attempted to filibuster the measure, the government moved a guillotine motion to restrict the time spent
in committee, but was defeated largely at the hands of its
own backbenchers. This coincided with the loss of Labour's
overall majority in the Commons due to by-election defeats
and defections. Facing a possible defeat in a Conservative-
sponsored confidence motion, Jim Callaghan made a deal
with the Liberals, who were no keener than Labour on
the prospect of an election at that time. The Lib–Lab Pact
allowed the Callaghan government to survive a confidence
motion by twenty-four votes and gave it the opportunity to
introduce the Scotland Bill (and a separate Wales Bill) – new
devolution legislation – later that year.

SNP MPs moved amendments to strengthen the proposed
assembly but without success, and opposed amendments
designed to weaken it with varying degrees of success. But
the biggest challenge came when the 40 per cent rule, a device
never previously or since used in a referendum in the UK,
was successfully introduced. This meant that the government
would have to lay an order in Parliament repealing the legislation, killing off devolution, unless the majority vote in the
proposed referendum also constituted 40 per cent of the eli-
gible electorate. This was the price that the government paid

to opponents of devolution in return for support for the bill. Since turnout in Scotland had been only 61.7 per cent in the 1975 EEC referendum, lower than in the previous general election, the 40 per cent rule would prove to be a high hurdle.

But by this stage the SNP had, in the words of MP Gordon Wilson, 'invested so much in the creation of a Scottish assembly' that it would have been difficult to withdraw support (Wilson, 2009, p. 185). The Conservatives' opposition to devolution had been hardening and the electorate would have found it difficult to understand why the SNP had changed its mind. In September 1978, the Liberals withdrew from the pact with Labour, creating a precarious situation for the government. Opinion polls suggested a comfortable win for supporters of devolution, even if the 40 per cent hurdle still looked unlikely to be cleared. Polls also placed Labour ahead of the Tories, and Callaghan was tempted to go to the country when the Lib–Lab Pact ended but, rather like Gordon Brown at a similarly favourable moment in 2007, the Prime Minister confounded expectations by deciding against calling an election. Like Brown, he soon had reason to regret the decision. Labour's poll lead dissolved over the ensuing 'winter of discontent', undermining the government and boosting the Conservatives, the principal opponents of devolution, as the referendum on 1 March 1979 approached.

Having had little choice but to campaign for devolution, the SNP played a full part in the 1979 referendum. It invested considerable resources in its campaign, which was led by Margo MacDonald and Stephen Maxwell, deputy party leader and campaign director respectively. Both would pay a price in the SNP for close association with devolution.

Despite a series of electoral setbacks the previous year when the party failed to win any of three parliamentary by-elections, saw its poll rating slump and suffered defeats in local elections, there were high expectations within the SNP as the referendum approached. Opposition to devolution within the party was almost invisible at this time, although it still existed on the margins. Labour, meanwhile, was more deeply and more openly divided (Macartney, 1981, p. 18). It did not help reassure voters fearful that devolution might lead Scotland on the 'slippery slope to separatism', as opponents suggested, that the party most united in its support was the one that saw it as merely a 'stepping stone' to independence. Towards the end of 1978, polls showing around 70 per cent support for devolution had given grounds for optimism but support for constitutional change – as often in referendum campaigns – was gradually whittled away (Bochel and Denver, 1981, p. 143).

The eventual result was a devastating blow to the SNP. A slight majority (51.6 per cent) voted for devolution but this amounted to only 32.9 per cent of the electorate. The government was legally bound to lay a motion before Parliament to repeal the legislation to establish the Scottish assembly. However, its MPs were not bound to vote for the repeal. The referendum result created a headache for both the Callaghan government and the SNP. Neither wanted an election as each looked set to lose seats and faced the prospect of the victorious Conservatives under Margaret Thatcher removing devolution from the agenda altogether. A majority could have been constructed against repeal had Labour been united but the extent of the split, unknown at the time outside a small group in the Labour government, ruled that out. A leading opponent of devolution supplied the Prime Minister with a list of thirty-eight Labour MPs who had signed up to repealing the Scotland Act. On the day after the referendum, Callaghan had told the Scottish Secretary:

> ... there would be great difficulty in taking Labour Members of Parliament along with the Government if it sought to introduce the Assembly. The important thing was to keep the Party together, rather than to come to a deal with the SNP. That might mean a General Election, but that was preferable to the prospect of a disunited Party. (National Archives, 1979)

The government's tactic was therefore to 'play for time' and leave the SNP to 'simmer along' and hope to cobble together a majority, including Ulster Unionist MPs, in any confidence vote.

The SNP's National Council, its key decision-making body between annual conferences, met days after the referendum and demanded that the Labour government 'honour its manifesto commitment' now that a majority of voters had supported the establishment of the assembly. Failing that, it recommended that its MPs should 'seek an early general election' in an attempt to force the hand of the Labour government. But the party was divided on tactics. A majority of MPs wanted to call the Prime Minister's bluff, but two MPs and a majority on the national executive committee feared forcing an election that would probably lead to a Tory government. There was a tension in the bicephalous leadership of the SNP, with the MPs and national executive pulling in opposite directions. Communication between the two groups broke down as the party struggled with its response to events. In the end, the SNP was in no mood to offer a lifeline to Labour. An ultimatum was issued to hold a vote on the repeal of the devolution legislation within a fortnight.

This attempt to force Jim Callaghan's hand failed. The SNP MPs then supported a successful no-confidence motion and contributed to bringing down the Labour government. All eleven SNP MPs voted against the government, though two would subsequently regret the decision. During the debate, Jim Callaghan accused the SNP and Liberals of walking into a trap and famously suggested that this was the 'first time in recorded history that turkeys have been known to vote for an early Christmas' (House of Commons, 28 March 1979). At the election, Christmas duly arrived for nine of the SNP's eleven MPs. The SNP's vote fell from over 30 per cent in October 1974 to 17.3 per cent and it lost twenty-nine deposits (the bar for which was then set at 12.5 per cent of the vote in that seat), having lost none at the previous election.

Devolution had been, in Gordon Wilson's (2009) words, a 'danse macabre' for the SNP. It left the SNP feeling cheated and distrustful of Labour and devolution. The SNP had ended up arguing for another's party's policy while that other party had been deeply divided on the matter. This would be *the* formative political experience for a generation of SNP activists that would inform their thinking for many years. The party had been out-manoeuvred. A myth grew that would be repeated ad nauseam, and continues to be thrown in the face of SNP activists, that the party was to blame for the election of Margaret Thatcher. Hostility between Labour and the SNP intensified. But these events only re-opened a fissure inside the SNP that had always existed. Those who had argued against devolution at the Motherwell conference in 1976 felt vindicated. Many of those who had taken a different position were careful to reposition themselves and adopted a hardline stance, while those closely associated with devolution suffered in internal contests. Knives were out for the devolutionists after the general election. This focused mainly on Margo MacDonald, the party's deputy leader and most prominent figure. Personality clashes and the usual petty jealousies added to the tension. Despite being the best-known SNP politician and a gifted communicator, MacDonald was kept as far from the media spotlight as possible in the run-up to the election. With a slump in support

as the election approached, all the ingredients were there for
dissent, denunciations and recriminations.

THE '79 GROUP

When the SNP had failed to advance in by-elections in 1978,
Helen Liddell, Labour's Scottish general secretary, had suggested that the SNP 'bubble had burst'. So it seemed in
1979. Infighting started over the summer months between
the general election and the SNP's annual conference. With
two seats and over half a million votes, the party had secured
some 'Short money' but much less than it had before the election. Staff in party headquarters had to be laid off. Interest
in the party declined and it struggled to get media attention other than for the fractious internal debates that invited
unwanted coverage.

Despite the different tendencies inside the party, the SNP
had little previous experience of organised factions. As one
study of factions in political parties written around this time
expressed it, such organised groups within a party will often
have connotations of 'illegality, if not malevolence and pathology' (Beller and Belloni, 1978, p. 6) and that was true here. In
August, a faction was set up that called itself the '79 Group,
which agreed three key aims at its first meeting: independence, socialism and republicanism (although it would remain
divided on republicanism and had varying interpretations of

socialism). It attracted a number of key figures on the left including Margo MacDonald and Stephen Maxwell. Much subsequent commentary would focus on the group's socialist and republican goals, leading to suggestions that a left/right tension had come to dominate the party's internal politics. However, the key to understanding the group and reactions to it at this time is a paper presented at this first meeting that advocated a gradualist approach and rejected fundamentalism. While there were some left/right tensions, predictably given that the SNP was truly a broad church in this respect, it was devolution that caused most divisions.

When Billy Wolfe decided to stand down as party chair, a position he had held since 1969, the '79 Group decided to put up Stephen Maxwell for the post, as well as a slate of candidates for other roles. Their opponents included Gordon Wilson, one of the two remaining MPs, and Willie MacRae, who would later become a leading figure in Sìol nan Gàidheal, another but very different faction. Wilson was the party establishment candidate and was careful to distance himself from the failed devolution strategy. MacRae would become something of a mythical figure in nationalist circles following his death in 1985, which led to conspiracy theories on the nationalist fringe suggesting he had been killed by British secret services. Wilson won easily with 530 votes to Maxwell's 117 and MacRae's 52 votes and would hold the post unopposed for the next eleven years. Margo MacDonald faced a contest for the deputy leadership for the first time since she had taken up that position five years before and was also heavily defeated. Douglas Henderson, one of the recently defeated MPs, outpolled her by 450 votes to 169. Henderson was on the party's right wing but he won despite this rather than because of it. He had been quick to adopt a hardline position on devolution and this contributed to his victory. Gordon Wilson himself also sounded more hardline during this period than before or since. So, although these results were setbacks for the '79 Group, it was gradualism rather than socialism that was defeated. At the same conference, resolutions supporting the primacy of the public sector in regenerating the economy and demanding that oil revenues should be used to tackle poverty rather than fund tax cuts were passed easily, and ran directly contrary to the emerging Thatcherite message across Britain.

This was a period of internecine strife and electoral weakness for both the SNP and Labour, but the former lacked the advantage of a large core vote. Both parties' internal battles were fought out at their annual conferences. In 1981, the '79 Group appeared to make progress when three of its members were elected to senior office. One of these was Jim Sillars, the former Labour MP. Frustrated at the Labour government's lack of progress on devolution, he had set up a separate Scottish Labour Party (SLP) in 1976 (Drucker, 1978) and joined the SNP in 1980, having lost his South Ayrshire seat a year earlier. Alex Salmond, another member of the '79 Group, was elected to the party's national executive for the first time.

The group had identified three key resolutions at the conference: supporting a 'real Scottish resistance and defence
of Scottish jobs' involving direct action 'including political
strikes and civil disobedience on a mass scale'; another rec-
ognising the 'failure of the private sector' and supporting an
enlarged public sector; and a third supporting 'armed neu-
trality', reversing the party's support for NATO membership.
Jim Sillars spoke in the civil disobedience debate: 'Sacrifices
there will be. People will be hurt ... it will be unpopular at
first ... We have to be prepared to accept that the cell doors
will clank behind some of us' (Mitchell, 1996, p. 225).

Perhaps not surprisingly, the '79 Group drew particularly
on younger SNP members, notably students, for its support.
However, its prominent senior figures also ensured that it
attracted considerable attention. The group's critique of the
1979 debacles was simplistic. Its view was that working-class
Scots were much more likely to have voted for devolution
and therefore ought to be the SNP's target. This required,
they felt, a clear left-of-centre message rejecting any 'catch-
all' strategy. For some SNP members, the '79 Group was little
different from the Militant Tendency in the Labour Party.

The 1981 conference turned out to be the apogee for the
group. Gordon Wilson gave Sillars responsibility for the civil
disobedience policy, in a move subsequently interpreted as
handing Sillars a rope with which to hang himself. Six SNP
members – all from the '79 Group – broke into the Royal High
School building, the planned site of the Scottish Assembly in

October 1981. All six were charged with vandalism and the party was ridiculed by its opponents and the press. A plan for a mass demonstration the weekend after the break-in was abandoned. The group's opponents inside the party pounced. A number of senior members, including party president Robert McIntyre and Winnie Ewing, now an MEP, set up a counter faction, the Campaign for Nationalism. Its sole purpose was to provoke a confrontation at the 1982 conference and have the '79 Group proscribed. This forced Gordon Wilson's hand. He moved an emergency resolution at the conference that would ban all groups within the party, threatening to resign if it was not passed, and won support from almost 80 per cent of delegates. *The Scotsman*'s political editor wrote a 'Lament to the Seventy-Niners after R. Burns', commemorating the dead at the 'Battle of Ayr, 5 June 1982':

> *Scots, wha hae wi Winnie bled,*
> *Scots, wham Sillars ne'er has led,*
> *Better tae be dead than Red*
> *in the SNP!*
> *Now's the day tae grasp for powr,*
> *Stamp oot a' thon Left-wing showr,*
> *And see proud Gordon triumph owr*
> *Thon vile Conspiracie!*

The '79 Group had only about 200 members at the time of its demise but it had attracted a lot of attention. The Scottish

Socialist Society, with members from other parties and none, was set up in an attempt to get round the ban. But the SNP leadership told its members on the Society's national committee that they would be expelled if they persisted with Socialist Society membership. Margo MacDonald jumped before she was pushed and resigned from the party of which she had been deputy leader only a few years before. Kenny MacAskill, who would later become Justice Secretary from 2007 to 2014, and Alex Salmond found themselves temporarily kicked out of the party as the 1983 election approached. All this did not augur well for the election that saw Mrs Thatcher returned with an increased majority. Nothing in recent local and by-election performance had given grounds for optimism. The SNP was unprepared for 1983, with few candidates adopted until the last minute. The party's vote share slumped to 11.8 per cent and fifty-three out of seventy-two deposits were lost. The only bright spot was that the party held – and indeed increased its vote share in – both of its two remaining seats.

CONSTITUTIONAL CONVENTION

The 1983 election had a similar effect on the SNP as it did on Labour. It did not remove dissent but it reminded the party of the existence of the electorate. Two months later, Wilson proposed a series of policy changes that would prove important long-term for the SNP. He sought to reverse the party's opposition to NATO membership, to back membership of the European Communities and to adopt a more conciliatory attitude to devolution. Wilson also started to refer to the SNP as a 'left of centre' party, a term that former '79 Group members and opponents could agree on.

Significantly, membership of NATO and the EC cut across the fundamentalist/pragmatist division over devolution. Winnie Ewing and Jim Sillars, bitter opponents in recent internal battles, could unite in favour of Wilson's initiative and Europe would prove an issue that helped to close wounds. Having been strong supporters of European integration in the 1950s, the party had become critical of the EEC in the 1960s and campaigned against membership in the 1975 referendum. Attitudes changed in the 1980s for a variety of reasons. The EC was seen as a loose international organisation with no single dominant force and, as such, much less of a threat to Scottish autonomy than a centralised UK. Jacques Delors's vision of 'subsidiarity' within a 'Social Europe' appeared, or at least was perceived in the SNP, to be sympathetic to Scottish nationalism. The party had to edge slowly towards a pro-EC position given the strong opposition in fishing communities that gave considerable support to the SNP. By 1988, though, the party had adopted 'Independence in Europe' as its rallying cry. It was thought to be among the most successful slogans in the party's history (Macartney, 1990, p. 35).

The party's 1979 conference had resolved firmly not to 'engage in any more dealings in assemblies, devolution or meaningful talks'. Such dealings were seen as a blind alley or even a trap by most delegates. The SNP wanted independence and nothing less. However, while Gordon Wilson had ridden the wave of anti-devolution sentiment to become party leader, he subsequently took a more moderate approach. A combination of continuing internal divisions and changing electoral context meant that intransigence became harder to sustain. At its 1984 conference, the SNP gave support to the principle of an elected constitutional convention. This policy had little prospect of implementation at the time, given the lack of support from other parties, but it marked another stage in the SNP's gradually softening attitude towards devolution.

The decline of the Conservatives at the 1987 election in Scotland, while they remained dominant in England, led Labour and the Liberal Democrats to embrace the idea of a constitutional convention. During the 1983–87 parliament there had been much speculation on the implications of what Bob McLean, a leading Labour home ruler, called the 'Doomsday scenario': a further decline of Scottish Tory support while the party won another Commons majority. This was exactly what happened: the Conservatives returned to office with another landslide but lost eleven of their twenty-one seats in Scotland. These were not propitious circumstances in which to introduce the poll tax, legislation that had been passed in the dying days of the old parliament. In Scotland, the tax was widely perceived as an imposition by an alien government. Coming after the closure of Gartcosh steel mill, seen as a symbol of Scottish heavy industry, and the decline of many other traditional Scottish industries, the poll tax was portrayed as evidence of a government that was out of touch and uncaring. What was emerging in the minds of a large section of the electorate was that the Conservatives were anti-Scottish.

The SNP was not alone in portraying the Tories in this way. Labour too played the Scottish card (Mitchell, 1998). However, the SNP proved particularly adept at exploiting the poll tax issue, finding it a source of unity, distraction from the ongoing rift over devolution, and new electoral support. Following the 1987 election – a mixed bag for the party, in which it lost both its existing seats but won three others, including Banff and Buchan, where Alex Salmond was first elected to the Commons – the poll tax came to dominate SNP thinking. The party considered two options for resistance – non-registration and non-payment – and opted to support the latter. It had hoped to shelter under an all-party campaign but it soon became clear that, while individual Labour politicians would back non-payment of the poll tax, Labour's official position would be less radical. The SNP decided to make non-payment its main platform in the 1988 local elections and doubled its share of the vote and its number of councillors. While remaining well behind Labour, the SNP moved into second place ahead of the Conservatives (who recorded their worst performance up to that point).

Later that year, the SNP overturned a huge Labour majority to win a by-election in the symbolically important seat of Glasgow Govan. The winning candidate, Jim Sillars, was now married to Margo MacDonald, who had won the same seat in a 1973 by-election. The SNP vote share increased by 38 points and national polls suggested that the party was once more on the electoral march. Robust opposition to the poll tax had helped to dispel any lingering impression of the SNP as 'tartan Tories'. Citing this issue, Dick Douglas, Labour MP for Dunfermline West, defected to the SNP in 1990 and the party also picked up new members, including many who had drifted away after 1979. Labour was pushed slightly onto the defensive, vying with the SNP to be the most anti-Tory party in Scotland.

One way for Labour to assert its credentials in this respect was to firm up its commitment to devolution as a bulwark against Tory policies. A cross-/non-party Campaign for a Scottish Assembly (CSA) had been set up in 1980 in an attempt to keep the issue alive. In July 1988, the CSA proposed the establishment of a constitutional convention to draw up a scheme of home rule. While similar in some ways to the proposal endorsed at the SNP's 1984 conference, the CSA's proposal differed in terms of the composition of the convention. Crucially, it preferred indirect rather than direct election. This meant a major advantage to Labour, which, with fifty of seventy-two Scottish seats at Westminster, would comprise the large majority of those represented. Although the CSA looked to achieve greater balance by also allowing the parties to nominate members, it was clear that Labour would still dominate the proposed convention and, after some hesitation, Labour agreed to be involved. The SNP had to decide whether it too would come on board.

At a time when their party's support was on the increase, many SNP figures saw in the convention a means by which Labour and others would undermine the case for independence. As so often in the SNP's history, a surge in poll ratings led many to think that independence was just around the corner. The decision over whether to take part in the convention opened the old fundamentalist/pragmatist fissure. Gordon Wilson consulted key figures over a weekend to ascertain views but failed to contact Alex Salmond, his deputy and the person most likely to support participation. The announcement was made that the SNP would withdraw from discussions on the establishment of the convention without Salmond's consent, which placed him in the difficult position of having to accept this or disagree publicly. Having been through the SNP's civil war only a few years before, he had no appetite for a further battle and decided to line up with others in the leadership. The SNP national executive then backed this decision with only one dissenting voice. A final decision was taken at a National Council meeting – one of the best-attended and most heated in many years – in Port Glasgow in March 1989. The party had backed its leadership and found itself portrayed as having returned to fundamentalism. And Alex Salmond, who would take over as leader a year later, could be portrayed in the same way, even if his private instincts were for a more pragmatic approach to the convention.

At the SNP's 1991 conference, Alex Neil, who had followed Sillars into the SNP from Labour via the Scottish Labour Party and was by then an SNP vice-chair, announced that the party's slogan at the forthcoming election would be 'Scotland Free by '93'. The expression on Alex Salmond's face said it all. This was not a decision that the leader had agreed to. However, many in the party shared Neil's ebullience. Polls pointed to a hung parliament and to an SNP advance. Within a fortnight in January 1992, three developments fed the hubristic mood. A debate on the constitution organised by *The Scotsman* in Edinburgh's Usher Hall attracted considerable attention, with Alex Salmond putting in a strong performance. Then a poll for ITN suggested support for independence was at 50 per cent and, in turn, the Scottish edition of *The Sun* came out in favour of independence.

If hubris had its customary aftermath, this had much to do with the electoral system. As in 1974 and 2015, expectations of a hung parliament boosted the SNP's relevance and, in turn, its vote share by 7.4 points up to 21.5 per cent. But the party ended up with just 4 per cent of Scottish seats – the same three that it had won in 1987. The Conservatives not only held onto all their seats but gained a seat from Labour and increased their vote share by a couple of points. And their majority at Westminster meant that the constitutional convention's scheme remained a draft with no prospect of implementation during that parliament.

Tensions eased inside the SNP with no immediate prospect of devolution and with the removal of Sillars, who had lost Govan, from front-line politics (although he would continue to comment from the sidelines). The focus shifted to Labour. Its new leader, John Smith, had been opposed to devolution when he first entered Parliament but became a firm supporter after being given responsibility for the issue under Callaghan in the late 1970s. Smith died less than two years after becoming leader but ensured that there was no Labour backtracking on its commitment to devolution. Tony Blair, his successor, was no enthusiast but was not prepared to re-open the debate within his party. However, he did insist that there should be a referendum with two questions: the first on the principle of devolution and the second on whether the devolved institutions should have tax-varying powers. This was a controversial strategy which led to the resignation of John McAllion as a Labour front-bench spokesperson on Scottish affairs. Blair's approach was a response to the campaign against devolution waged by Michael Forsyth, the first leading Scottish Tory in at least a generation to have offered a serious fightback against opponents. Forsyth focused on the tax-varying element in Labour's proposed devolution scheme, describing it as the 'tartan tax'. Given New Labour's determination to shed its image as a tax-and-spend party, this attack hit a sensitive spot and the two-question referendum was the response. There was consternation among supporters of devolution at this dilution of Labour's commitment. It was inevitable that the promise to hold a referendum would awaken old fears that this was a device to ditch the commitment to devolution. However, the two-question referendum allowed Labour to go into the 1997 election formally committed to devolution while also spiking Forsyth's guns and thus winning votes from those sceptical about devolution and its fiscal implications. This and much else worked for Labour at that election, the party taking fifty-six of Scotland's seventy-two seats with 45.6 per cent of the vote, its largest share since 1966. The Tories lost all of their Scottish seats and fell behind the SNP in share of the vote for the first time since October 1974. Underlining how far the party was at the mercy of the electoral system, the SNP's vote share barely changed but its seat tally doubled.

Legislation to hold referendums in both Scotland and Wales was passed within months of the general election, with the votes held in September 1997. The SNP moved an amendment to add a third question on independence but this was predictably rejected in Parliament. The party therefore had to decide its position on the devolution referendum. Public opinion meant that opposition looked likely to be fruitless. There was strong support for devolution and clear if slightly more equivocal public support for tax-varying powers.

With no 40 per cent rule, devolution looked within sight. Shortly after the general election, the SNP leadership signalled a willingness to be involved in the referendum campaign for devolution. The SNP national executive unanimously supported a motion recommending support for devolution in the referendum. In early August, this was debated by the party's National Council and received overwhelming support. Senior figures Gordon Wilson and Jim Sillars remained critical and stood aloof from the campaign, still fearing that devolution was a trap. But SNP members played a prominent part in the referendum and Salmond was the key figure in the campaign, working under the umbrella organisation Scotland FORward. In the end, 90 per cent of SNP backers – the largest proportion of any party's supporters – and 93 per cent of those favouring independence voted Yes–Yes in the two-question referendum (Denver et al., 2000, pp. 158, 161). The SNP had travelled far from its suspicion of, even opposition to, devolution eighteen years before. This was Alex Salmond's greatest achievement in his first period as leader.

FUNDAMENTALISM AFTER DEVOLUTION

The establishment of the Scottish Parliament brought an end to the key tension that had afflicted the SNP from its foundation. But devolution was not independence and a new set of challenges emerged. How could the SNP transform devolution into independence? Was it a trap that would make independence impossible to achieve as Jim Sillars warned? As shown in the graph at the beginning of Chapter 5, devolution did not trigger any increase in public support for independence. Fears were soon expressed that George Robertson might have been partly correct when, in 1995, he had famously predicted that devolution would 'kill nationalism stone dead'. And old divisions over devolution resurfaced over the question of whether and how it might be used as a base on which to make the case for independence.

Hardliners were particularly aggrieved by the party's manifesto for the first election to the Scottish Parliament in 1999 for a number of reasons. Independence was placed tenth in a list of the party's ten major commitments. The leadership was criticised for having lost sight of independence in its bid to become Scotland's largest party in the early days of devolution. As discussed in the previous chapter, this criticism was not unjust: the party's leadership, and Alex Salmond in particular, was indeed focused primarily on winning power in the Scottish Parliament. The commitment was not to independence itself but to a referendum on the issue. Prior to devolution, the party had maintained that an SNP majority of Scottish seats in the Commons would be a sufficient mandate to negotiate independence. There had long been a view among many senior figures that this would not be enough and that a referendum would be necessary. Since the SNP had supported the use of referendums in its draft constitution for an independent Scotland and had taken an enthusiastic part in the recent devolution referendum, it was not a major leap to commit to a referendum on independence in its 1999 manifesto. The leadership had, however, to confront those who thought that a commitment to a referendum diluted the party's commitment to its central goal. Kenny MacAskill, future Justice Cabinet Secretary, played a key role in winning party activists over to the argument for a referendum. The SNP leadership knew that support for independence was lower than the party's potential support within the electorate. And it had learned from Labour in 1997 that a referendum promise would allow the party to reach beyond its core support without simply shelving its commitment and thus alienating its base.

Alex Salmond stood down as leader in 2000 after a decade in the post. As with other MPs who had stood for the Scottish Parliament, he had held onto his seat in the Commons. While others combining the jobs of MSP and MP after 1999 stood down from the Commons at the next UK election in 2001, Salmond instead resigned from Holyrood and stood again only for Westminster. His presence in Holyrood would undoubtedly have created difficulties, or at least awkwardness, for his successor. The leadership election was fought along familiar SNP battle lines, with John Swinney presented as the pragmatist and Alex Neil the hardliner. Swinney had an easy victory, winning 67 per cent of the delegates' votes. The SNP placed more emphasis on independence in its campaign in 2003 but this seemed to satisfy neither hardliners nor voters, the party losing eight seats in the second election to Holyrood. John Swinney faced a leadership challenge from Bill Wilson, a fringe candidate barely known even in SNP circles, who argued that the SNP leadership had 'watered down our commitment to independence, the one clear difference between ourselves and the other parties' (Constitution Unit, 2003, p. 35). Swinney won over 80 per cent of the vote but had been bloodied in the process and felt under pressure to deliver both greater emphasis on independence and a better electoral performance, not obviously compatible objectives at that time.

In September 2003, Alex Neil asked for a ruling from the Scottish Parliament's Presiding Officer on whether a bill proposing a referendum on independence would be within the Parliament's legislative competence. This was provoked by Swinney's insistence that an SNP administration would introduce such a measure within three years of coming to power. George Reid, formerly an SNP MSP but by now Presiding Officer, dodged the question stating that, under the terms of the legislation creating the Parliament, there was no mechanism for making speculative rulings. However, he added that 'if a bill was submitted for introduction I would, as you know, offer a view on legislative competence as required under the Scotland Act' (Constitution Unit, 2003, p. 31).

Swinney was keen to avoid the problem of having a bicephalous leadership with the NEC and parliamentary

leadership in conflict. His main legacy as leader was to transform the internal party constitution, again learning from
Labour and other parties' experiences. A special conference
in spring 2004 agreed a series of reforms: streamlining the
NEC; fewer national office bearers; the introduction of a central membership system; one-member-one-vote (OMOV) in
internal elections, including for the leader, deputy leader and
parliamentary candidate selections; more stringent require-
ments for contesting leadership positions; and the formal
creation of a party leader in place of a party convenor or
chair. These proposals had been criticised by the hardliners
who feared that removing power from the activists at party
conference would dilute the commitment to independence.
To placate such critics, Swinney proposed to change the aims
as stated in the party's constitution from 'self-government'
to 'independence'. This was akin to a Clause IV moment in
reverse: while appearing to harden the party's ideological
stance, all it did was to formalise a position the SNP had
long adopted. What it did not do was to specify what the
SNP understood by independence. Although it was clear that
the party's change of policy on Europe in the 1980s had also
implied a redefinition of the notion, independence would not
be formally defined until the publication of the party's White
Paper 'Scotland's Future' in November 2013.

Swinney stood down as leader after a poor performance
in the 2004 European elections. However, he had created
the conditions that would allow his successor to be elected

with far less prospect of being challenged by some fringe figure. Power within the party had moved decisively away from
activists both upwards to the leadership and downwards
to the membership. The result tended to bear out May's
(1973) law of 'curvilinear disparity', according to which
a party's activists are more ideological, radical or hardline
than both its leadership and its ordinary party members.
Although Swinney's leadership had seen constant rumblings
of discontent about a dilution of the party's commitment
to independence, the old fundamentalist/pragmatist tension
hardly registered in the 2004 leadership contest.

There was pressure on Alex Salmond to stand again but
he was very reluctant, initially attempting to kill off speculation and pressure by announcing that 'if nominated I'll
decline. If drafted I'll defer. And if elected I'll resign' (BBC,
2004). But pressure mounted and when it looked likely that
Nicola Sturgeon, his preferred candidate, might be defeated,
he agreed to stand. Sturgeon made way for him and stood
with his support for the deputy leadership. Salmond won
easily, taking three-quarters of the votes in the first SNP
leadership contest under OMOV. He defeated Roseanna
Cunningham, an old '79 Group colleague, and Mike Russell,
who had served as SNP chief executive during Salmond's
first period as party convenor. Nicola Sturgeon was returned
as Salmond's deputy, winning 54 per cent of the vote. The
incoming leader's pitch emphasised the continuing priority of
winning power at Holyrood: he announced that he was 'not

just launching a campaign to be SNP leader ... I am launching my candidacy to be the First Minister of Scotland'.

Salmond's election was a rare pivotal moment in politics.
Internal SNP discontent all but subsided, with the exception
of a few malcontents on the fringe, despite the absence of
any evidence that independence had moved up the party's
agenda. The commitment to a referendum on independence
was again included in the SNP's 2007 manifesto but, without any likely coalition partner with which to build majority
support for that referendum, the link between voting SNP
and Scotland becoming independent seemed broken. As discussed in the previous chapter, this was crucial in aiding the
party's transition to government.

Once elected as a minority government, the party
conducted what it called a 'national conversation' on the
constitution. This was a means of keeping independence on
the agenda so as to satisfy the hardliners, while suggesting
to a sceptical electorate that the party was also interested
in listening rather than simply dictating on this issue. The
White Paper on the constitution that the party produced in
July 2007 (Scottish Executive, 2007) was noticeably light
on independence, at least from a party for which this was
supposed to be its primary goal. This reflected the development in SNP thinking on Scotland's constitutional status. Its
opening page included Parnell's dictum that 'No man has
the right to fix the boundary of the march of a nation'. This
emphasis on fluidity was usefully ambiguous: it challenged

any notion that devolution was the end of the story but it also suggested that, even if independence was not the conclusion of this particular 'conversation', this did not preclude that outcome at some future time. In his preface, Alex Salmond made no claim to having a mandate for independence but noted only that people had voted for 'further development of the way we govern ourselves' and that, while the governing party supported independence, others supported 'increased devolution, or greater responsibility for taxes and spending, or federalism'. There were eighty-eight references to independence but ninety-two to devolution, and only one of the six chapters addressed independence. From a fundamentalist point of view, this was a deeply timid document. Nothing so hesitant could ever have been produced by the SNP at any time in the long years in opposition. For the leadership, though, it was the only document possible within a few months of first being elected to power, especially as a minority government.

This timidity might have been challenged had the SNP's opponents sought to call its bluff. Scottish Labour leader Wendy Alexander briefly supported an independence referendum – urging the SNP to 'bring it on' – but was effectively overruled by Gordon Brown. The SNP therefore had little choice other than to use its period in office to build credibility with the electorate and work to create a reputation for competence. Electoral success, combined with the possibility of rewarding MSPs – including those, like Alex Neil, known for taking a harder line on independence – with ministerial posts, silenced criticism of this strategy.

EVERYTHING CHANGES

There were thirty-five references to independence and eight to its continuing referendum commitment in the SNP's 2011 manifesto. This compares with seventy-nine references to health and ninety to education in the manifesto entitled 'Re-elect a Scottish government working for Scotland'. The passage on a referendum did not appear to anticipate a referendum any time soon: 'As we have seen, with your support we can take forward our proposals for a referendum, and we can also, in the meantime, make the current Scotland Bill better' (SNP 2011). The emphasis on governing rather than constitutional change was noted by the electorate. The SNP's majority will have been owed in part to the fact that the constitutional question had fallen by eleven points between 2007 and 2011 as 'the single most important issue when deciding how to vote in the election' among the electorate (Carman et al., 2014, p. 99). Until the result of the election became known, a referendum looked no more likely than four years before.

The pre-election polls in 2011 had – eventually – suggested an easy win for the SNP but the overall majority came as a surprise to almost everyone, and independence came to dominate the next few years of Scottish politics. We can only speculate what might have occurred, or indeed what might yet occur, had the SNP continued to win elections but without making progress towards independence. The likelihood must be that a growing band of activists would have raised concerns. But the outcome of the 2011 election, as much a surprise to the SNP leadership as to anyone else, meant that they had no option other than to demand a referendum. The party's activists had been waiting for this moment and expected payback for the remarkable self-discipline displayed over the previous four years.

Polls suggested that the timing was not right. We saw at the beginning of Chapter 5 that only one in four Scots supported independence when the SNP was re-elected in 2011. That proportion was larger but not much so when pollsters asked a straight Yes/No question rather than about respondents' preferences among a range of options. There was speculation that Alex Salmond would have been happier had London refused to permit a referendum and allowed him to take advantage of – and indeed urge – a backlash against London. The Prime Minister himself might have been more obstructive had the polls suggested that the Union was at greater risk. Within days of the 2011 election, David Cameron agreed that the UK government would not block a referendum. And Salmond's approach was to take advantage of the opportunity at least to gain more powers. Contrary to his image as a gambler who would stake his and Scotland's future on a risky wager, he was keen on an each-way bet. He actively pursued a referendum with three options – independence, the status quo and more powers – confident that Scotland would end up with something other than the status quo. Notably, there was no dissent in his party on this. However, when it became clear that London would not countenance a third option and sought to polarise the debate, it was his deputy rather than Salmond who was more determined to accept what was probably the inevitable binary choice. A consultation on the matter conducted by the Scottish government came out emphatically supporting a Yes/No referendum. Independence was now firmly on the agenda.

CHAPTER 7

GRASPING VICTORY FROM THE JAWS OF DEFEAT

It became a commonplace after the referendum to remark that the losers were behaving like winners while the winners were behaving like losers (e.g. MacDonald, 2014). This seems a lot less puzzling once we distinguish between the referendum and the campaign. 'Yes' lost the referendum but won the campaign by a distance. And, since the first of these was widely expected, it was the second that captured more attention. The referendum itself was for all but the last couple of months regarded by many as a foregone conclusion. Commentators – and not only those opposed to independence

– wondered about the size of the 'No' victory and the extent of damage to the SNP. These expectations meant that what was ultimately a clear 55/45 defeat was widely seen as a moral victory among supporters of independence. Their case had proved more convincing to undecided voters, even if there were ultimately too few of them to swing the outcome. And the sense of momentum was all the stronger because of the conspicuous gap between 'Yes' and 'No' in terms of the enthusiasm and energy of campaigning and public support.

The aim of this chapter is not to provide a narrative of the referendum campaign. That would need a book in itself and plenty have beaten us to it (Blain et al., 2016; Macwhirter, 2014; Pike, 2015). Our concern is with the SNP's role, strategy and relationship with the broader 'Yes' campaign during the referendum, and its attempt to capitalise on that surge of enthusiasm and engagement once the result was in.

NEGOTIATING THE EDINBURGH AGREEMENT

The Scottish government invited opinion on the conduct of the referendum over the months following the 2011 election and was particularly interested in whether people wanted a third option on the ballot paper. Polls had long shown that when the 'more powers' option was available, the public consistently and convincingly preferred it to both the status quo and independence. A straightforward independence versus status quo referendum would be a gamble and looked at the time an especially poor gamble for the SNP. During the 2011 Scottish Parliament election campaign, amid all the vote intention polls were a cluster asking about votes in a (then) hypothetical referendum and the average result was 55 per cent for 'No', 31 per cent for 'Yes' with 14 per cent 'Don't know's. It was no wonder that the SNP downplayed the issue during that campaign.

Indeed, the Scottish government had already made clear during the previous parliament that it was willing to include a question on more powers as well as independence on the ballot paper (Scottish Government, 2010). This was repeated in its consultation after the 2011 election, when the SNP government stated that it 'will listen carefully to the views and arguments put forward on this issue in response to this consultation' (Scottish Government, 2012, p. 6). In fact, the SNP leadership encouraged submissions favouring the inclusion of more powers on the ballot paper. But no political party was willing to engage and, while a number of organisations and individuals were arguing for more powers for Holyrood in its many guises – devo max, devo plus, fiscal autonomy, federalism, fiscal federalism – none emerged with sufficient support and momentum to ensure that it became a serious contender for inclusion. So there was no clarity and agreement on what any third option should be. Less than 40 per cent of those who responded to the consultation and commented on this issue opposed including any intermediate option on the ballot paper, and, even among those who favoured it, many agreed that 'more powers' needed to be defined (Griesbach et al., 2012, p. 26).

Even had there been a groundswell of support for a third option on the ballot paper, London was not ready to concede. Including 'more powers' was seen as some ploy either to win independence by the back door or to allow the SNP to save face and emerge partially victorious. The polls mentioned above suggested that the referendum was an opportunity to defeat, even humiliate the SNP. Bearing in mind the tendency for referendum campaigns to see a late swing in favour of the status quo (Renwick, 2014), pushing support for independence below 30 per cent was not regarded as being out of the question. This was thought – by some within the SNP as well as its opponents – likely to lead to a repeat of the kind of internal blame and recrimination that occurred after 1979.

The constitution was a reserved matter under the terms of the devolution legislation. Theoretically at least, Parliament at Westminster remained sovereign and could deny the Scottish Parliament the right to hold an independence referendum. Lawyers debated this at length but at the end of the day this was a political rather than legal matter. Had the Prime Minister decided to try to block the referendum or, more likely, had a private citizen challenged its legality, this would have created a potential crisis and inflamed the situation. There was never much doubt that a referendum would be held. What remained at issue was how and when it would be conducted. In January 2012, London agreed to remove any legal impediment to hold the referendum so long as the terms agreed were 'fair, legal and decisive'.

Agreement was reached between the two governments on the conduct of the referendum in October. The Edinburgh Agreement meant that the Scottish government could pass legislation for an independence referendum. This included setting its date so long as this was before the end of 2014, determining the franchise, deciding on the question wording so long as it was a single question with two options, and specifying campaign finance rules subject to agreement with the Electoral Commission. EU citizens would be allowed to vote and the Scottish government would consult on extending the franchise to sixteen- and seventeen-year-olds, a longstanding policy of the SNP. The assumption in many quarters was that this was designed to maximise support for independence. If so, it was based on the flimsiest evidence. There had been evidence that the SNP had benefited in the past from disproportionate support among young voters and there were grounds to expect a similar pattern in backing for the relatively radical step of independence. But the age differences in voting patterns were never likely to be stark, and the number of sixteen- and seventeen-year-olds was too small in any case to make much difference. Nonetheless, the concession of this extension of the franchise showed that the UK government did not anticipate a close result.

WINNING THE CAMPAIGN

In March 2013, First Minister Salmond announced that
18 September 2014 would be the date of the referendum.
But the campaign was already well under way. An immediate
danger for the SNP was seeming isolated or even isolationist
on the 'Yes' side. While umbrella campaigning organisations
would be established on each side, parties play a significant
part in referendum campaigns (Sniderman, 2000) and voters'
adoption of their parties' positions is the 'quintessential short-
cut in direct democratic votes' (Kriesi, 2005, p. 139; Hobolt,
2007, p. 160). Given the extent to which Scotland's constitutional status had been a central issue in Scottish politics and
the parties had well-known positions on the subject, the danger for the SNP was that the combined forces of Conservative,
Labour and Liberal Democrats were not only greater but
would leave the SNP portrayed as isolationist, not just in
its constitutional preference but in its approach to political engagement. This had happened in the past. The party
had been left in this situation when it had turned its back on
cooperation, as in the years of the constitutional convention.

The SNP responded in two ways. First, it sought to encourage the view that the campaign for independence was more
than an SNP campaign. The old distinction between the
national movement and the SNP had become blurred since
the party's electoral rise. In order to maximise the vote for
independence, the SNP had to encourage the view that the

national movement was far wider than the party. While the Greens also officially supported independence, the electorate could be excused for being unaware of this at this time given the priority given by that party to other issues. The Electoral Commission requirement that a single umbrella group should be established for each side was an opportunity to tackle this problem. Yes Scotland was launched in May 2012, chaired by former Labour MP and Independent MSP Dennis Canavan, with Blair Jenkins, a former senior broadcaster unaffiliated to any party, as its chief executive and Stephen Noon, SNP staffer and former special adviser to Alex Salmond, as chief strategist. Yes Scotland spawned a number of local and other bodies. Success required that the campaign should be seen as more than an SNP campaign while simultaneously drawing on the SNP's campaign professionalism and sophistication.

The second response was to turn the challenge of isolation into an opportunity. The uneasy alliance within Better Together, the cross-party campaign for the Union, offered the SNP an opportunity to point to what it could portray as Labour–Tory complicity. Just as the SNP had suffered from voting against the Labour government in 1979 and the Lib Dems had recently suffered from coalition with the Tories, so too might Better Together damage Labour. SNP branches across Scotland compiled instances of Labour politicians campaigning with the Tories. The icing on the cake came when Alistair Darling, chair of Better Together and former

Labour Chancellor of the Exchequer, received a standing
ovation at a Scottish Tory conference fringe meeting.

The SNP was aware that the media would be overwhelmingly against independence and it had to find ways of getting
round this. Its recent election victories had been delivered by
an efficient, disciplined central machine. The referendum had
to be different: the need to overcome the massive advantage
its opponents enjoyed in the media required direct means
of reaching out to the wider public. And the duration of
the campaign also allowed for an emphasis on registering
voters and encouraging turnout. This is part of the reason
why campaigning for independence took on such a strongly
'bottom-up' character. Yes Scotland's claim to have been
Scotland's largest ever grassroots political campaign, while
hard to prove, has a ring of accuracy rather than hyperbole
(see also Geoghegan, 2014). However, even if the scale and
intensity of local mobilisation was largely unplanned, the
grassroots nature of the 'Yes' campaign emerged partly by
design and partly by necessity given its disadvantages in the
media and in terms of mainstream party support.

Yet this was still clearly and strongly an SNP campaign.
Table 7.1 shows, for a range of 'Yes' campaign activities, the
breakdown by party allegiance (based on a question asked
in February 2014) of those involved. In each case, SNP supporters provided the large majority of campaign activity.
That is not just because they make up the majority of independence supporters. As the bottom row of the table shows,

existing SNP loyalists made up only 54 per cent of the 'Yes' vote, but they accounted for more – often comfortably more – than 54 per cent of every type of 'Yes' activist during the referendum campaign.

TABLE 7.1: GRASSROOTS 'YES' CAMPAIGNERS
BY PARTY IDENTIFICATION

	PARTY IDENTIFICATION				
	LABOUR	SNP	OTHER	NONE	*N*
Tried to persuade family, friends or colleagues to vote 'Yes'	14	66	8	12	*353*
Registered online as a supporter of Yes Scotland	11	71	6	12	*200*
Signed up to the 'Yes' Declaration of Support for Independence	10	74	6	10	*241*
Displayed a poster	12	75	6	8	*196*
Attended a public meeting/ speaker event	18	61	8	13	*157*
Joined a local campaign group	4	75	6	15	*68*
Delivered leaflets or canvassed voters	11	69	11	8	*61*
Joined a political party	4	80	16	0	*25*
Voted 'Yes'	20	54	9	17	*718*

Sources: British Election Study Internet Panel Wave 1; Scottish Referendum Study

Meanwhile, amid all this frenzied activity on the ground, the SNP leadership remained in charge at the top. The publication of the Scottish government's White Paper on independence in November 2013 attracted considerable

international as well as national media interest and formed
the basis of understandings of what was being proposed.
And when there were differences on the 'Yes' side – as, for
example, when the Greens and Dennis Canavan took a different view from the SNP on Scotland's post-independence
currency – then it was the SNP's view that prevailed.

The lengthy campaign gave 'Yes' time to challenge the
large majority against independence, but it carried risks.
As Scotland's governing party, the SNP feared that it would
do its cause and the party's prospects at the next Holyrood
elections little good if it was seen to focus exclusively on the
referendum. There was also the danger that Alex Salmond
would be over-exposed in a long campaign, and so his engagement with the campaign began low-key and increased as
referendum day approached. In September 2012, Nicola
Sturgeon was moved from her post as Cabinet Secretary for
Health and Wellbeing to take up the Infrastructure, Invest-
ment and Cities portfolio, while retaining her position as
Deputy First Minister and leading the SNP's referendum
campaign. She was already a well-known figure but the referendum would put her in the spotlight over a sustained
and challenging period. She participated in televised debates
(with Johann Lamont, Scottish Labour's leader, Anas Sarwar,
Scottish Labour's deputy leader, and Alistair Carmichael, the
Lib Dem Scottish Secretary), even though the debates between
Salmond and Darling attracted most attention.

A key feature of the 'Yes' campaign that came directly

from the SNP's electoral toolbox was the emphasis on positive campaigning – or, at least, being seen to fight positively while accusing opponents of a negative approach. Since its 2007 Holyrood campaign, the SNP had insisted that its success was owed in large measure to its positive message and there is evidence from voting studies of at least some truth in that claim (Pattie et al., 2011). Positive campaigning was obviously easier for a 'Yes' than a 'No' campaign but, even allowing for that inherent difficulty, Better Together still did a very poor job of rebutting claims of negativity – never more so than when its own director of communications let slip that his team was (jokingly, he insisted) referring to its campaign as 'Project Fear' to describe its campaign (Pike, 2015). In the Scottish Referendum Study's post-referendum survey, 63 per cent of voters described the Yes Scotland campaign as positive and 59 per cent felt that it was successful in 'putting forward a clear vision of the Scotland it wants'. The corresponding proportions for Better Together were 23 per cent and 33 per cent. Given that 55 per cent voted 'No', it is clear that at least some within this group were unimpressed by their own side but felt some grudging respect for the 'Yes' campaign. The losers looked a bit like winners, and vice versa.

When Dennis Canavan addressed the SNP conference in March 2013, he told the delegates that he kept being told that they had a mountain to climb, but added, 'I like climbing mountains.' This was received with rapturous applause

and summed up the attitude of many in the SNP. Only in
the closing weeks did the polls suggest that there was any
likelihood of a victory for independence, but 'Yes' activists
never gave up throughout months of flatlining opinion polls.
Dissatisfaction with Yes Scotland was occasionally expressed,
but the SNP leadership was largely spared.

BEHAVING LIKE WINNERS

The contrast for the SNP with the 1979 devolution referendum was stark. In 1979, the SNP was campaigning for
another party's policy in the expectation of an easy win. In
2014, the SNP were fighting for its own policy with conviction
and unity – 95 per cent of SNP identifiers voted 'Yes', a larger
proportion even than the 'No' vote among Conservatives –
and was doing so against the odds. Although there had been
two polls recording a 'Yes' lead, the second of these released
less than a week before the referendum, all the rest, including
the final five to be published in advance of polling day, put
'No' ahead. So, although the final result was a comfortable
majority for remaining in the Union, this was not a shock.
Nor did it feel especially comfortable compared to the easy
win that had been anticipated when the campaign began and
had still looked on the cards even two months before polling. This created a post-referendum dynamic very different
from that in 1979. If losers started to behave like winners,

then that is because that is how they quickly came to feel. Campaigners for independence took a sense of achievement from the startling 85 per cent turnout and were overrepresented among those claiming the referendum to have been a triumph of political deliberation. The Scottish Referendum Study survey asked respondents whether they agreed or disagreed that 'the independence debate has given ordinary people a say in Scotland's future'. Forty-four per cent of 'Yes' voters strongly agreed compared to just 29 per cent from the victorious 'No' side. As this perhaps implies, few supporters of independence believed that the issue had been put to bed. Alex Salmond's immediate announcement that he would stand down as First Minister and leader of the SNP ensured that his party could move on from the defeat and remove an obvious target for his opponents.

Supporters of the Union were relieved but many were also unhappy. The SNP had been defeated but not humiliated and the more staunchly Unionist regretted the price that had been paid for victory. In a last-minute effort to pull back support, the three main UK parties had combined to promise more powers. Each party had at least hinted at this before, but the way it was presented offered little room for backpedalling and, crucially, included a timetable for providing more powers. 'The Vow' that appeared on the front page of the *Daily Record* on 16 September committed these parties to 'extensive new powers' and to the 'continuation of the Barnett allocation for resources, and for the powers of the Scottish Parliament to raise revenue'. In effect, more powers had replaced the status quo on the ballot paper at the last moment.

Over the days following the referendum, SNP headquarters became aware of something they had not anticipated. Each week, the party would check membership levels. The official charged with doing so was surprised to see a significant increase in online applications in the hours after the announcement of the result. Figure 7.1 shows the sheer scale of this surge in membership numbers. (Note that the scale of the horizontal axis is stretched to chart the more rapid changes since the referendum. Maintaining equal spacing would make those changes look still more dramatic.) Membership had been steadily increasing up until the referendum, reflecting the party's electoral success, but it was the result of the referendum that triggered the sudden acceleration. Membership doubled within a week of polling day. The sharp increase in SNP members became a news story, in turn fuelling further increases. The Scottish Greens saw a similar surge (albeit on a much smaller scale) from 1,500 members before the referendum to nearly 9,000 by April 2015, underlining the appetite among 'Yes' supporters for continued political involvement. And, while the rate of increase had slowed by the end of the year, membership continued to grow more quickly than it had prior to the referendum and the 2015 general election brought a further boost, with two thousand more members joining the SNP in the twenty-four hours following Nicola Sturgeon's participation in one of the televised leaders' debates.

FIGURE 7.1: SNP MEMBERSHIP NUMBERS, 2003 TO JUNE 2015

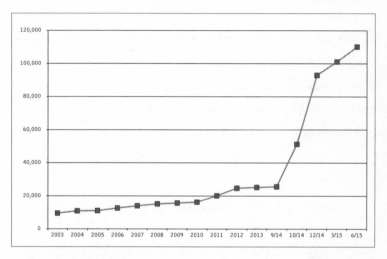

Source: Electoral Commission

Three other things about that upward curve in Figure 7.1 are worth noting. The first is that the SNP's membership, now amounting to more than 2.5 per cent of the Scottish elector-ate, makes it the kind of mass party not seen in the UK since the 1950s. Second, it is easily overlooked that this brings in a lot of additional income – and, in turn, expands the SNP's administrative and ultimately election-fighting capacity. The third point is that, given the 'bottom-up', grassroots nature of so much of the 'Yes' campaign that brought these recruits into the SNP, it is perhaps surprising that they have chosen membership of a political party as a means of remaining

engaged. The German sociologist Robert Michels coined the
phrase 'the iron law of oligarchy' to refer to the fact that
political parties, like other major organisations, inevitably
become more top-down and less democratic as they institu-
tionalise, progress and seek office. Today's SNP conforms to
that iron law. So we might wonder whether branch meetings,
circulated minutes and party lines will satisfy the participatory tastes of these new recruits – who now make up the
large majority of the membership. The implications of this
for the SNP are explored in the next chapter.

HANDOVER

Nicola Sturgeon was the only candidate nominated to replace
Alex Salmond as SNP leader and First Minister. Given her
standing in the party, there was never any serious doubt
that she would take over. Even if her previous post, that
of party deputy leader, is often little different from the
vice-presidential role that was famously described by one
incumbent as 'not worth a bucket of warm piss', Sturgeon
had not been a bit-part player. She had been a close second
in command and was one of the few Cabinet Secretaries
who could successfully challenge Alex Salmond over matters beyond her formal ministerial responsibility.

Following a strong and successful leader is not an easy
task. Taking over from Alex Salmond looked a little like

taking over from Alex Ferguson (which was still proving difficult at the time of writing). John Swinney had struggled to follow Salmond after the latter's first period as leader. In the event, however, the succession was smoother than even the most optimistic within the SNP could have anticipated. This is partly because, as noted in Chapter 4, Sturgeon was by this point a more popular figure across the electorate. Her overall ratings were weighed down by the polarising effect of the referendum campaign – no figure heavily involved could avoid rejection by the other side – but an average like–dislike rating of 4.7 on a 0 ('dislike a lot') to 10 ('like a lot') scale is high by politicians' standards, and both 'Yes' and 'No' voters showed a preference for the incoming over the outgoing leader.

Denied a leadership contest, Sturgeon instead set out on a tour of Scotland, addressing massive audiences, including twelve thousand people in Glasgow's Hydro arena in November. It is hard to distinguish any Sturgeon leadership 'bounce' from the generally buoyant mood among 'Yes' campaigners, and hard therefore to estimate whether any other successor would have drawn the same crowds. What is clear is that the energy and excitement of the referendum looked to have been transferred to the SNP's new leader.

Alex Salmond announced he would stand for a seat in the Commons (where he had remained an MP until 2010) and stand down from his Holyrood seat in 2016. But if he imagined that a return to Westminster would provide him with an arena for continuing leadership then he had not taken account of the very prominent role that his successor would play in the general election. Sturgeon's standing was enhanced in the televised leadership debates and she had the opportunity to introduce herself to voters UK-wide who might have known Salmond but were unaware of the SNP's new leader. This was confirmed by the Conservative campaign poster in which the original version showed Ed Miliband inside Alex Salmond's pocket but which was then updated to show Sturgeon instead.

Her performance in the debates was widely praised. The message was clear: the SNP was pivotal in the election and its MPs would both vote to 'lock the Tories out' and put pressure on Westminster to deliver on 'The Vow'. She challenged Labour to decide whether it would work with the SNP or allow the Tories back into power. However it played in England, Miliband's failure to come down unequivocally in favour of locking out the Tories simply seemed to confirm to Scots that the Labour–Tory Better Together alliance remained intact. Similarly, the *Daily Mail*'s description of Sturgeon as the 'most dangerous woman in Britain' might have had appeal in England, but left most voters in Scotland bemused.

In Chapter 4, we identified three means by which leaders can have an electoral effect: through sheer likeability, through respect for their abilities, and through their effect on their parties. At one time, Sturgeon might have been expected to score more highly on the second than the first: her public image was rather guarded and stern, and Salmond himself was prone to reinforce this when praising her for keeping him in check (*Scotsman*, 2011). But she has become an increasingly relaxed as well as an increasingly confident performer. This, alongside the general easing of post-referendum tensions, may explain why Sturgeon has proved increasingly likeable during her tenure as leader. In a November 2015 poll which included another like–dislike scale, her average rating had climbed to 5.4 – above the neutral point and up to the same heights as Salmond in 2011. Apparently, according to YouGov's 'Profiles' analysis in the same month, this kind of rating was enough to crown Sturgeon 'the most popular and widely appreciated living person among the Scottish public – four places ahead of the Queen' (Dahlgreen, 2015). There is an unexpected link between these two contenders for Scots' affections, judging by one of Lord Ashcroft's focus groups in Scotland in the run-up to the 2015 general election. When asked who would play the title role in *Nicola Sturgeon: The Movie*, group members agreed by 'common consent' that that role would go to Helen Mirren – or, if it had to be a Scottish actress, then Elaine C. Smith, perhaps best known outside Scotland as the long-suffering wife of Rab C. Nesbitt (Ashcroft and Culwick, 2015).

The rather different choices of Helen Mirren and Elaine C. Smith suggest a politician who has succeeded in appearing as a stateswoman without becoming disconnected from her west of Scotland roots. The first part of this points to respect for Sturgeon's leadership abilities, respect which is confirmed

in various poll series. YouGov have asked Scottish respondents whether they think Sturgeon is doing well or badly as
First Minister, and in the most recent poll in February 2016
she had a net rating of +40. The 70 per cent who thought
that she was doing 'very' or 'fairly' well clearly includes
plenty of people who have not voted and will not vote SNP.
And Sturgeon polls particularly well on questions asking
about trust in her to work in Scotland's interests and, in particular, to deliver more powers for the Scottish Parliament.

As yet, the indirect effects of Sturgeon's leadership have
been limited for three reasons. The first is simply that she
has not been very long in the job and so has had limited
time to leave her mark on the party's image and strategy.
Second, it is not clear that that mark would be so different from Salmond's in any case. Sturgeon was so closely
involved during Salmond's leadership that she was never
likely to be planning any major change of direction thereafter.
Third, compared to the other major parties in Scotland, the
SNP's image when she took over was a broadly positive one
and so the kind of complete overhaul that was the primary
indirect effect of, say, Tony Blair's leadership was not necessary. However, as discussed in the next chapter, Sturgeon's
SNP now faces some strategic decisions about how to balance its 'safe pair of hands' approach to Holyrood elections
with its large and growing band of members and voters
who want visible progress towards independence. Assuming
that she holds to what has been her unremittingly cautious

approach over recent years, Sturgeon will leave a distinct imprint on the choices and image of the post-referendum SNP.

Meanwhile, it is worth noting what looked like one immediate such imprint. According to polls at the 2015 election, the gender gap in SNP support had narrowed almost to non-existence, suggesting that the party under Sturgeon had remedied any image problem in terms of its appeal to women voters. However, since that gap is showing signs of re-opening in the 2016 polls, any interim judgement here should be hesitant.

CAPITALISING ELECTORALLY

The term landslide has been used to describe past British elections – 1983 for the Tories and 1997 for Labour, for example – but none compare with the Scottish results in 2015. The SNP won fifty-six (95 per cent) of Scotland's fifty-nine seats with 50 per cent of the vote. Labour's reverse was on a par with that of the Progressive Conservatives in Canada in 1993, when Kim Campbell's party lost 156 seats to be left with only two. In Chapter 1, we looked at the sharp break that this election marked from previous Westminster contexts. Our concern here is with the role of the referendum in taking the SNP from six to fifty-six.

The party knew that, provided it could win over the 45 per cent who had voted for independence, then the remaining

55 per cent would be split between its opponents, enabling big SNP gains, and perhaps even a clean sweep, under first-past-the-post. The leadership considered how best to achieve this. One idea was to allow supporters of independence outside the party to stand as Yes Scotland rather than as SNP candidates. These would then be endorsed by the SNP, in much the same way as in the 'coupon election' after the First World War, when candidates were endorsed as official representatives of the coalition government with a letter or coupon. This was opposed by Nicola Sturgeon, who was willing to relax the rules on how long a candidate had to have been a member of the party but insisted on standing candidates under the SNP banner. She was similarly clear that she would be the leader of the party's contingent in the House of Commons. What emerged as the key criterion in the selection of SNP candidates proved to be the level of activity during the referendum. Longstanding members, including some who had stood for the party in the past, were pushed aside by newcomers who had served a short but intense apprenticeship during the referendum.

At the same time as harnessing the momentum and energy of the referendum, the SNP had to avoid suggesting that it was proposing another referendum or indeed that independence was on the agenda at all. Instead, 'The Vow' ensured that its opponents were also still talking about extending devolution and allowed the party an ideal opportunity to fight on its preferred territory of standing up for Scotland without needing to mention independence. The relentless line was that only a vote for the SNP would ensure that its opponents delivered the powers promised in the closing days of the referendum. In announcing his resignation the day after that referendum, Salmond had already insisted that the referendum result provided the opportunity to 'hold Westminster's feet to the fire on the "Vow" that they have made to devolve further meaningful power to Scotland'.

Another advantage of focusing on the last-minute 'Vow' was that, because it had been signed by all three major Westminster parties, the SNP was able to tar all of its significant opponents in Scotland with the brush of reluctance to deliver on this pledge. This was also a reminder to 'Yes' voters of Labour's alliance with the Conservatives, and thus made it more difficult for Labour to regain sympathy among those of its former supporters who had voted for independence. For their part, the Conservatives had predicted that the referendum would give them a bounce and hoped that Friends of the Union, set up by the party but open to anyone, would provide a channel to recruit new members and increase the party's support. Aligning themselves closely with Labour might have offered the Conservatives a means of finally decontaminating the party in Scotland. In the event, it simply contaminated Labour.

A related feature of the campaign that worked to the SNP's advantage was its anti-austerity message. Spending cuts were portrayed not simply as draconian and unnecessary but also as inflicted on a Scottish public that had long rejected their Conservative sponsors. Labour's discomfort and equivocation on austerity helped the SNP. While the issue territory was reminiscent of elections in the 1980s, Labour was no longer successful in portraying itself as the leading anti-Tory progressive force. The SNP had now adopted that mantle – and so successfully so that it was able virtually to wipe Labour from Scotland's electoral map.

DEEP UNDERCURRENTS

While the independence referendum was the critical juncture in the process of the SNP replacing Labour as Scotland's dominant party at Westminster, the undercurrents had been evident for some time. Over the past fifty years or more, a combination of structural changes in the Scottish economy and society and a weak response to these changes had left Labour exposed. However, while parallel changes in England left the party more vulnerable to the Conservatives in Westminster elections, in Scotland the Tories had ceased to pose a meaningful threat. So even – or perhaps especially – when out of power at Westminster, Labour could always portray itself in Scotland as the party that would battle for Scottish interests against the Tories. Devolution changed the picture because it generated a political arena in which Labour's new leading rival, the SNP, was far harder to defeat on that 'standing up for Scotland' criterion. Labour maintained a reasonable reputation in that regard during the early years of devolution, not least because it was the party that had delivered the Scottish Parliament in the first place. But the good working relations between the Labour governments in London and in Edinburgh, initially seen as an electoral advantage for the party over its more divisive SNP rival, eventually led to suspicion that Labour in Scotland was controlled by the leadership at Westminster. The SNP grew fonder of jibes about 'London Labour'.

Shortly after the referendum, Johann Lamont announced she was standing down as Scottish Labour leader, having been largely marginalised in the referendum campaign. In stating that the Labour leadership at Westminster treated the party in Scotland 'like a branch office of a party based in London', she seemed to confirm SNP criticisms. This problem was unlikely to be remedied for Labour by the subsequent election of Jim Murphy as its new Scottish leader. Although Murphy stood down from Labour's shadow Cabinet at Westminster and insisted that he would stand for election at Holyrood, he had been close to Tony Blair for many years and was easily portrayed by the SNP as personifying 'London Labour'.

Labour was unsure how to respond to polling evidence that the SNP were pulling well ahead. Many Labour figures believed that the overhang from the referendum would disappear as the general election approached, as voters concentrated on a straight choice between David Cameron and

Ed Miliband to enter Downing Street. But the widespread expectations of a hung parliament scuppered that and, in any case, the referendum cast a long shadow. Murphy realised that many Labour voters had gone against the party in the referendum and promised to appoint a 'Yes' supporter to his team, insisting that Labour was open to supporters of independence. Gordon Brown hoped that Labour could press the 'reset' button, allowing Scots to move on from 'obsessing about the constitution' to 'focus on improving people's lives'. But the referendum campaign had not simply been about the constitution. The issue of independence had become intertwined with everyday public policy concerns, and Better Together's success on macroeconomics and currency issues had not been matched in areas like job creation and funding of public services. Like some voters, some issues also seemed to be shifting from Labour to the SNP via 'Yes'.

A vivid illustration of the electoral impact of the referendum, and of the SNP's success in winning over 'Yes' supporters, is provided by Figure 7.2, which shows the proportion of independence supporters voting SNP – or, in the case of 2016, intending to vote SNP – at recent elections to Westminster and Holyrood. In previous UK general elections, the party had failed to win over more than about two thirds of its natural base of independence supporters. In 2015, partly due to its renewed viability as emphasised in Chapter 1 but also due to the impact of the referendum campaign, around nine out of ten voters who favoured independence

backed the SNP. The same proportion of 'Yes' voters, according to a YouGov poll in February 2016, planned to vote
SNP in the Holyrood election in May. The SNP's ambition
of holding on to the 45 per cent from 2014 was fulfilled
almost completely.

FIGURE 7.2: SNP VOTE SHARE BY SUPPORT
        FOR INDEPENDENCE, 2001–16

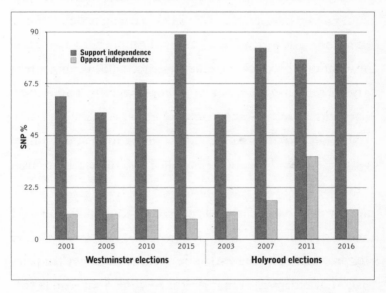

Sources: British Election Studies, 2001–10; British Election Study Internet Panel Wave 6;
Scottish Social Attitudes, 2003; Scottish Election Studies, 2007–11; YouGov, 2016

But if the effect of the referendum was to bring referendum and election voting so closely into line, there was an
obvious flip side for the SNP. Its recent success in Scottish
elections, especially in 2011, was owed in large part to winning over voters who oppose independence. Some of these

then followed the party into 'Yes' voting, but plenty of others did not. Could the SNP regain the support of the latter after a long and polarising referendum and then a Westminster campaign which, if not explicitly focused on independence, was hardly conciliatory to Unionists? The darker columns in Figure 7.2 suggest that the answer is 'no'. In 2015, at by far the most successful Westminster election in the party's history, the SNP actually lost ground slightly among those opposed to independence. This did less damage than it might have done given that that group, once a large majority, is now barely 50 per cent of the electorate. But it points to a post-referendum realignment of voting that has a negative as well as a positive side for the SNP.

The big question for 2016 is whether that realignment will extend to a Holyrood election. The SNP had no proven record of winning over opponents of independence in Westminster elections, but it had enjoyed striking success among these voters in 2011. When it comes to 2016, we are at the time of writing dealing with vote intentions rather than votes cast. That complicates matters because it is conceivable that the ensuing campaign, focused on who governs at Holyrood rather than with what powers, will revive the conditions of 2011 and re-extend the SNP's reach among those who still oppose independence. As things stand, however, 2016 looks much more like 2015, not just in terms of the SNP's dominance among 'Yes' voters but in its failure among 'No' voters. Consider two groups of people. The first voted SNP in 2011 but 'No' in 2014. The second did not vote SNP in 2011 but voted 'Yes' in 2014. According to the long-term Scottish Election Study/Scottish Referendum Study panel, only 24 per cent of the first group plan to return to the SNP in 2016, while 67 per cent of the second group plan to vote for the party – probably for the first time in a Holyrood election – in 2016.

CONCLUSION

Electoral success for the SNP, whether the breakthrough in the 1970s or the major gains under devolution, had always been about going beyond independence. In Chapter 5, we described the party's strong 'valence' credentials in recent years – its popular leader, its governing credibility, the tone of its campaigning, and its reputation for standing up for Scotland within the existing constitutional arrangements – which are relevant for voters of all constitutional preferences. All of this boosted the SNP's vote share in two ways. First, it provided reasons for those opposed to independence nonetheless to support the SNP. Second, it removed reasons why some of those in favour of independence had not been voting SNP.

Up to and including 2011, the second of these was less important to the party than the first. There were too few supporters of independence to deliver electoral success, even if the party could monopolise that group. Success on anything approaching the scale of 2011 would require a long reach into the large majority who opposed independence.

That has now changed. While there is nothing like the clear and consistent majority for independence that the SNP would want to see before taking the gamble of another referendum, there is equally little sign of support for independence falling from the high 40s. The strategic ground facing the SNP has therefore shifted dramatically. The referendum has made it more difficult but also less necessary to appeal to 'No' voters. A near-monopoly over supporters of independence is currently enough for landslide victories under first-past-the-post at Westminster and for likely majorities under the not-quite-proportional system at Holyrood. In Scottish Parliament elections, the main threat might even come from the Greens, currently the party best placed to deny the SNP that monopoly over the 'Yes' vote. In the next chapter, we examine in more detail where the referendum has left the SNP in terms of its electorate, its membership and its strategic dilemmas.

CHAPTER 8

PARTY OF GOVERNMENT OR PARTY OF INDEPENDENCE?

T he SNP won its Holyrood majority by being a safe pair of hands on the tiller. It won its Westminster majority having rocked the constitutional boat almost to the point of capsize. In this final chapter, we examine the tension between the SNP's radical goal of independence and its more mainstream goal of retaining office in Scotland. That same tension is at play within the party's electorate, its membership and its leadership. The party's successes in Scottish Parliament elections and increase in membership since Salmond's return to the leadership were achieved partly by downplaying the constitutional issue and thus attracting voters across the board, including many who opposed independence. Yet the post-referendum surge in support and especially membership came from those inspired by the 'Yes' campaign and impatient for constitutional change. There are differences at the top of the party, too, even if these have been subdued by electoral success. If the polls show an upturn in support for independence beyond the current mid-40s, that cautious consensus among the SNP's elite will again come under strain.

One purpose of the chapter, then, is to assess where the SNP – at various levels – wants to strike this balance between being a party of government and being a party of independence. A distinct but parallel question concerns the social and ideological profile of SNP support. Again, the SNP's advances under devolution were made across the social and demographic board, including progress among the middle-class voters it had found harder to attract in previous decades. This left it resembling a 'catch-all' party – that is, one that polls well across the electorate but risks lacking an obvious base in one group, community or class. By contrast, the 'Yes' vote was seen as having a more distinctive profile – clearly on the left and drawing from traditional Labour strongholds in the working-class and Catholic communities. Now that the SNP has won an unprecedented general election vote on the back of the independence referendum, a pertinent question is whether that success reflects a continued appeal across groups or a repositioning onto Labour territory.

This helps us to map the strategic ground facing the SNP's leadership as it approaches the 2016 election. We conclude by assessing how it will tread that ground, both in the short term and in the event that some 'material change' brings another referendum into view. A recurring question concerns the flip side of the success in converting 'Yes' votes into SNP votes in 2015 and, it seems, in 2016 as well. The party's majority in Holyrood was owed partly to those who opposed independence in 2011 and had not changed their minds by September 2014. Can the SNP hold on to – or win back – their support in this post-referendum electoral climate?

A NEW SNP ELECTORATE?

When the SNP made its first significant electoral gains, in the 1960s and early 1970s, the most distinctive feature of its vote was its lack of distinctive features. At a time when Labour and the Conservatives still won support principally from their traditional class bases, the SNP, not surprisingly for a party whose vote was based on a national appeal, won its support from across classes (Miller, 1981; McCrone, 1992). The same was true of religion, with the exception of the SNP's – and any other party's – inability to threaten Labour's dominance among Scottish Catholics. Over the couple of decades leading up to devolution, the picture changed, but only slightly. The SNP had made conscious and assiduous efforts to boost its appeal to working-class and Catholic voters, helped by the strengthening association between Scottish national identity and left-wing – and especially anti-Conservative – political identity. In both cases, these efforts at first led only to small electoral gains. They left the SNP with a discernible class profile, the party polling slightly better among working-class than middle-class voters and among renters than owner-occupiers, and an improved showing but still lots of ground to make up among Catholics.

Perhaps partly because of this indistinct social profile, attention often focused instead on the age and sex of the party's voters. Two stereotypes became established: of the SNP as a party of young people in the 1970s; and of the SNP as a party of men in the post-devolution period. Like any such stereotypes, there was exaggerated truth in both. The size of the gender gap was rather variable and sometimes – as in the 2003 Scottish Parliament election (Curtice et al., 2009, p. 106) – it more or less disappeared (although, since a gender gap of two points is within most surveys' margin of error and therefore might disappear and then reappear as a gap of four points just by statistical chance, changes over time were hard to track and explain). Nonetheless, there was a systematic advantage for the SNP among male voters – which, at its most pronounced, was one of the larger gender gaps in elections across Western democracies. As discussed in Chapter 4, it can be attributed in large part to greater male support for independence. With age, meanwhile, the stereotype may have been misleading because it mistook a generational for a life-cycle effect. In other words, perhaps the 1970s SNP polled heavily among younger people not because those voters had the radicalism of youth but because they were raised into a very different political environment from those raised with experience of the British Empire, the Second World War, and more generally a time at which the major two parties were dominant. On the generational account, these voters would not simply desert the SNP as they reached the age of supposed political sobriety – but of course the party could not rely on the youth of the next political generation. And that is what happened: over time, the SNP's strongest showing would be in the middle-age groups as this generation moved through the life-cycle (see Table 8.1 below and also Brown et al., 1999).

As the party moved into the era of devolved elections, then, its vote had some demographic wrinkles but was otherwise very even across the sociological board. Then, when the party made big gains in 2007 and even bigger gains in 2011, these were also made across the board. In both elections, the party increased its vote appreciably among every demographic, social and economic category (Curtice et al., 2009, pp. 106–7; Carman et al., 2014, pp. 30–32). Where this left the SNP in 2011 is shown in the first column of Table 8.1. Some of the old differences persist – the party's

TABLE 8.1: VOTE SHARES BY SOCIO-DEMOGRAPHIC CATEGORY:
SNP 2011; 'YES' 2014; SNP 2015

	SNP HOLYROOD (CONST.) 2011 %	'YES' REFERENDUM 2014 %	SNP WESTMINSTER 2015 %	DIFFERENCE 2015 V. 2011	DIFFERENCE 2015 V. 2014
SEX					
Male	48	48	51	+3	+3
Female	43	42	48	+5	+6
AGE					
18–29	41	49	55	+14	+6
30–39	47	51	56	+9	+5
40–49	51	49	54	+3	+5
50–59	47	46	50	+3	+4
60+	44	39	45	+1	+6
RELIGION					
None	48	51	53	+5	+2
Church of Scotland	46	39	47	+1	+8
Catholic	40	54	55	+15	+1
OCCUPATIONAL CLASS					
AB	44	40	43	-1	+3
C1	42	42	50	+8	+8
C2	48	51	54	+6	+3
DE	48	53	58	+10	+5
CLASS SELF-IDENTIFICATION					
Middle	42	35	39	-3	+4
Working	46	49	56	+10	+7
HOUSING TENURE					
Owner	43	40	45	+2	+5
Renter	49	55	60	+11	+5
NATIONAL VOTE SHARE	45	45	50	+5	+5

Sources: Scottish Election Study, 2011; Scottish Social Attitudes, 2011; Scottish
Referendum Study, 2014; British Election Study Internet Panel Wave 6.

relative weakness among the middle classes, Catholics and the oldest voters – but these gaps, narrowing by the 2000s, look even smaller when the party was winning 40 per cent or more of the vote even in these categories of relative weakness. As lamented in Chapter 2, the 'astonishing lack of quantitative data collection on BME electoral participation in Scotland' (Peace and Meer, 2015, p. 26) means that we have only anecdotal evidence on ethnicity and voting. However, since the war in Iraq eroded Labour's popularity among Pakistani voters across Britain, and since that war was certainly no more popular in Scotland than elsewhere, we might reasonably infer that the SNP – vocal opponents of the war – has made ground in that community as well. In the 2011 Scottish Parliament election, at the time by far its strongest showing in any electoral arena, the party's vote was therefore remarkably uniform across Scottish society.

This stress on 'across-the-board' gains might seem strange given that the story of election night in 2011 was one of the SNP sweeping into Labour's working-class heartlands in Glasgow and surrounding areas. One might easily infer that the party made particular gains among working-class voters. That is misguided. The SNP did not gain *votes* disproportionately in those Labour heartlands. The party's list vote went up by 12.8 percentage points nationwide – and by 12.8 points in the Glasgow electoral region, barely different from the 12.2-point gain in the SNP's existing stronghold of north-east Scotland. In the same way as the party gained votes across the

sociological board, it also gained votes across the geographical board. The *seat* gains came from points south and west
because that is where they were to be taken. Of the fifty-two
Holyrood constituency seats that the SNP did not already
hold in 2011, thirty-seven were in Labour's hands, most of
these in the west, central or Glasgow electoral regions. Any
sweeping SNP gains would take a particular toll on Labour
and in those areas.

All this is of particular relevance given what happened
three years later. Comparison is confounded by the fact that
the referendum results were announced by local authority
area rather than by Scottish Parliament region, but even
rough comparison is enough to see that support for independence did not map onto support for the SNP. Certainly
the average 'Yes' voter in 2014 lived further south-west than
did the average SNP voter in 2011. Support for independence was below the national average in party heartlands like
Angus and Moray, but comfortably over 50 per cent in areas
like West Dunbartonshire, where Labour remained the largest party. (If we correlate the independence vote in a council
area with the parties' 2012 local election showings, the correlation is actually stronger for Labour than for the SNP.)
The implication was that, while 'Yes' in 2014 won the same
45 per cent share as the SNP had on the constituency ballot in 2011, these must have been rather different voters. By
comparing the first two columns in Table 8.1, we can see
how far this was true.

When it comes to socioeconomic characteristics, the 'Yes' vote was effectively a caricature of the SNP vote: it had the same working-class features but they were a little more pronounced. The same was true of its maleness, reinforcing the idea that the partisan gender gap was driven largely by greater support among men for independence. The features are a little more skewed when it comes to age and religion, however. The average 'Yes' voter is rather younger than the average SNP voter – perhaps because 'Yes' genuinely was a radical option, while an SNP vote is much less so these days – and, while Catholics remained somewhat resistant to the SNP in 2011, they were the warmest embracers of independence in 2014.

These results are exactly what would be expected given the differences across council areas in the percentage voting for independence. Whether we are talking about geographical or sociological territory, the 'Yes' vote moved further onto Labour ground than the SNP had managed even in 2011. Assessing the reasons for this is not our primary aim in a book about the SNP rather than about the referendum per se, but two points from the previous chapter are worth recalling. First, in its campaigning, 'Yes' made a sustained attempt to associate Scottish political interests and identity with the left and its traditional constituency. So the success on Labour soil is not surprising. Second, while turnout soared throughout Scotland, an increase on that scale could only be achieved by disproportionately mobilising those generally more inclined to abstain. This meant exactly those voters – not just the

youngest but also those from lower socioeconomic brackets
– who have typically been associated with Labour but whom
'Yes' won over in 2014.

For our purposes, all this raises two questions about the
SNP's prospects in 2015. Would the party be able to follow
in 'Yes's wake and reach those parts of traditionally Labour
Scotland it had failed to reach in 2011? And, if the SNP was
hoping to benefit by association in those areas that voted
'Yes' in 2014, would it also lose votes by association in those
areas – and among those people – who voted 'No' in 2014?
The remaining columns in Table 8.1 can answer these questions. Direct comparison with the other votes is disrupted by
the fact that, with the SNP winning 50 per cent of the vote
in 2015, we would expect the figures in that third column to
be higher on the whole anyway. This is not merely a statistical irritant, of course: the fact that the SNP vote was higher
in 2015 than in previous contests is already a sign that its
vote probably expanded socio-demographically rather than
simply shifting from one group to another.

Nonetheless, a quick scrutiny of those first three columns,
especially towards the bottom of the table, makes clear that
2015 has more in common with 2014 than with 2011. The
big differences in referendum voting by housing tenure and
social class – whether objectively measured by occupation or
subjectively measured by people's self-identity – are also evident in SNP voting in 2015. Significantly, the referendum also
seems to have served as a stepping stone for some Catholics

to move over to the SNP. The remaining data in the table confirm these points. The rightmost column shows the difference in each group between its 'Yes' share in 2014 and its SNP share in 2015. If this referendum vote and general election vote shared exactly the same socio-demographic characteristics, this would be a column filled with +5s (reflecting the overall difference in vote share). And, in fact, it is not so far off that. Not surprisingly, Church of Scotland affiliates found it rather easier to vote SNP than 'Yes', and the reverse is true of Catholics. But the overall profile of these two votes is remarkably similar given that we are comparing a referendum and an election.

By contrast, there is much more variation in the adjacent column. Between 2011 and 2015, the SNP made big gains among Catholic voters, manual workers and renters, but made no real progress among the oldest voters and Church of Scotland-goers and actually lost a little ground among the subjectively and objectively middle class. These losses were sufficiently small – within or close to the margin of error – that we can broadly confirm the suggestion above that the SNP's vote expanded within rather than shifting across society. Nonetheless, it is clear that this most recent expansion was not made across the board like the gains between 2007 and 2011; rather, it came off the back of the referendum and among those groups which had been likeliest to vote 'Yes'.

Regression analysis, as introduced briefly and used in Chapter 4, is useful here in two respects. First, it helps us to avoid 'double counting' when looking at the patterns in Table 8.1. When we say, for example, that the SNP struggled to make gains among the oldest voters and Church of Scotland-goers, these are overlapping groups such that we don't know whether the struggle was to win over pensioners (who happen often to be Presbyterians) or Presbyterians (who happen often to be pensioners). Regression allows us to see which characteristics are genuinely influential – that is, to distinguish causation from correlation. It turns out that age tends to trump religion while social class – especially subjective class identity – trumps housing tenure. Second, regression provides a measure of how much more accurately – in percentage points – we could predict voters' choices if we knew all of their characteristics from the table. These boosts in accuracy tend to be quite small, since there is a great deal more to voting than socioeconomic background and that is especially true in the case of the SNP, which continues to poll fairly uniformly across Scottish society. Here, though, we are interested in whether its electorate has become a little more distinctive and the answer is that it has. The improved accuracy measures are 3 per cent, 7 per cent and 6 per cent for 2011, 2014 and 2015 respectively. In words rather than numbers, then, the changes in the SNP's electorate leave it with a small but discernible skew towards younger and more working-class voters.

We would draw the same conclusion if looking at constituencies rather than individual voters. Figure 8.1 shows the correlations between various aspects of the socioeconomic profile of an area and its SNP or 'Yes' vote share in those three years. (The units differ in each case – seventy-three Holyrood seats in 2011, thirty-two councils in 2014 and fifty-nine Westminster seats in 2015 – but the correlations are nonetheless comparable.) The further each bar stretches from the central axis, the better that that characteristic distinguishes areas of SNP or 'Yes' strength and weakness. So bars pointing a long way leftwards mean a strong but negative correlation: that is, the more voters with that characteristic, the lower the SNP vote share.

FIGURE 8.1: CORRELATION BETWEEN CONSTITUENCY SOCIO-
DEMOGRAPHIC CHARACTERISTICS AND SNP/YES
VOTE SHARES, 2011–15

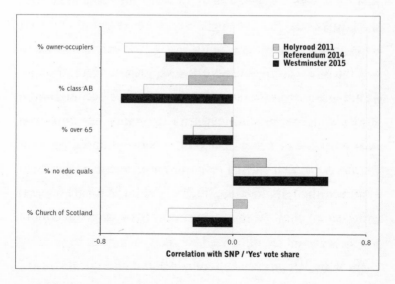

Sources: Census data and election results

This chart tells the same story as Table 8.1. While there were signs in 2011 of the SNP doing a little better in less middle-class areas, the differences were small – the shortness of the lighter-coloured bars are the manifestation of the SNP's across-the-board appeal in that year. By 2015, in contrast, the party had much more socioeconomically distinct strongholds – where there were few owner-occupiers (and more social renters), fewer people in professional and managerial occupations, fewer older people and more people with no educational qualifications. And it is clear that the referendum was the driving force behind this, given the similar patterns for 2014 and 2015.

If there is a difference between the results from individual voters (Table 8.1) and those from constituencies or areas (Figure 8.1), it is that the patterns seem more pronounced in the latter case. The SNP polls a little more strongly among working-class voters but quite a lot more strongly in working-class areas. Observers of British general elections such as Pattie and Johnston (2000) have noted something similar. While it was getting more difficult to predict an individual's vote from his or her social class, it was becoming easier to predict how a constituency would vote based on its social class profile. Labour seats in the urban north became ever safer, as did Conservative seats in the leafy south, as though voters were more influenced by the type of people around them than by their own characteristics.

Two explanations for this are highly relevant to the SNP in

recent years. The first is that voters are indeed influenced by those around them. 'People who talk together, vote together', as Pattie and Johnston themselves put it when demonstrating that two voters with exactly the same characteristics are quite likely to vote differently if one has a strongly Conservative social network or neighbourhood while the other's is strongly Labour. And the more intensively a network discusses politics, the stronger are the effects on its members' voting decisions. This is an important point in the wake of an independence referendum that made politics a recurring topic – welcome or otherwise – in many people's social interactions. The effect will have been a geographical polarising of opinion: 'Yes' neighbourhoods became more 'Yes', while 'No' neighbour-hoods became more 'No'. If these referendum votes then translated into votes for and against the SNP in the general election, we have an explanation of the pattern in Figure 8.1 whereby neighbourhoods already sympathetic to the SNP in 2011 became more pronouncedly so in 2015.

The second brings us back to viability, but this time at the local level. One reason seats become safer over time is because voters learn that 'around here, there's no point vot-ing for anyone else'. The reason the SNP gains in the west of Scotland in 2011 and especially 2015 were surprising was not because the kinds of people living in those areas had long proved allergic to the party. If anything, as we have seen, there was a working-class bias in the SNP electorate. And in no devolved election has knowing a voter's social class been much help in predicting whether he or she would vote SNP or Labour (Paterson et al., 2001, ch. 4; Carman et al., 2014, pp. 31–2). Socioeconomically, then, this was arguably just as much SNP as Labour territory. But *politically* it had always been Labour territory. Only once the SNP became a viable winner there, thanks to its rising tide across Scotland, did what we might call the 'natural' correlation between SNP vote share and social class characteristics emerge.

These results from 2015 led David Denver to conclude as follows: 'Despite winning 50 per cent of Scottish votes, then, the SNP is no longer a "catch all" party without a distinctive social base. Rather, in this election at least, it has taken over what were formerly the bases of Labour dominance in Scotland...' (2015, p. 19). While this is a neat summary, two caveats are worth noting. The first is that the SNP could be said to have had at least a discernible social base prior to 2014. Aside from the influx of Catholic supporters, the main effect of the referendum was to accentuate patterns that have existed at least since the 1980s, when Scottish national and working-class identities started to become entwined (McCrone, 1992, ch. 6; Bennie et al., 1997, ch. 7). If Scottish nationalism appealed disproportionately to certain groups even during 'peace-time', it is not surprising that that would intensify during a long referendum battle. The second caveat is to question whether the SNP has really lost its claim to be a 'catch-all' party. This term was always slightly misleading in that, while parties like New Labour and the German

CDU certainly shuffled towards the centre ground to expand their territory, they never 'caught all' either in terms of vote share or in terms of socioeconomic groups. Labour under Blair had a more middle-class electorate than it had ever had before, but it was still appreciably a working-class party in comparison to the Conservatives. Judging by Table 8.1, the SNP today is similar: it has a perceptible base but is by no means confined to it. Whether this constitutes 'catch-all' status is a definitional nicety. But if the SNP is not a catch-all party, then there are very few around.

A NEW SNP MEMBERSHIP?

The SNP won around 900,000 votes in 2011 and, of these, well over 700,000 stuck with the party in 2015. This overlap between the two electorates is one reason why the changes in Table 8.1 are not dramatic. New voters in 2015 were still outnumbered by the 2011 base. This is absolutely not true in the case of the party membership. Within just two weeks of the referendum on 18 September 2014, those joining since that date already outnumbered pre-referendum recruits by two to one (*Herald*, 2014), and Chapter 7 has already confirmed that this exponential growth continued. While the new voters might at most *reshape* the party's electorate, then, the new members had the potential to *transform* the profile of that membership.

Has such a transformation taken place? When a blogger reported that the 'surge in SNP membership is predominantly working class and broadly left wing' (Morrison, 2015), this was conjecture but squarely in line with received wisdom. These new members were brought to the party by a 'Yes' campaign that seemed to mark a break from conventional party politics and which was able to mobilise those sectors of society and geographical areas usually most reluctant to turn out. This has led many to infer that there was a similarly Heineken-like quality – reaching the parts that others cannot reach – to the SNP's surge in membership. On the other hand, membership of a mainstream party (as the SNP has now been for decades) remains a conventional rather than a radical form of political participation, and membership also remains a minority pursuit – even in the case of the much-expanded SNP. More than 90 per cent of those who voted SNP in 2015 have not joined the party, despite in many cases having been active within the referendum campaign. There are grounds to suspect that the minority that did join is unrepresentative of 'Yes' supporters in just the same way that party members – in the SNP (Mitchell et al., 2012) and more generally (Bale and Webb, 2015; Widfeldt, 1995) – are an unrepresentative minority within society, being more middle class, more middle aged, more educated and more male.

Now, courtesy of a recent internal SNP survey of the party's membership, we can compare the profiles of members who joined before and after the 2014 referendum (Table 8.2). When it comes to social class, the story is now a familiar one.

TABLE 8.2: SOCIO-DEMOGRAPHIC PROFILE OF SNP MEMBERS JOINING
BEFORE AND AFTER THE INDEPENDENCE REFERENDUM

	JOINED PRE-REFERENDUM %	JOINED POST-REFERENDUM %	ALL MEMBERS %
SEX			
Male	64	55	58
Female	36	45	42
AGE			
18–29	5	8	7
30–39	9	14	13
40–49	19	24	23
50–59	26	27	27
60–69	27	21	23
70+	15	5	8
ANNUAL HOUSEHOLD INCOME			
Up to £19,999	23	22	23
£20,000–£39,999	33	32	32
£40,000–£59,999	22	21	22
£60,000+	22	24	23
OCCUPATIONAL CLASS			
AB	69	65	67
C1	9	10	10
C2	11	11	11
DE	11	13	12
CLASS SELF-IDENTIFICATION			
Middle	36	32	33
Working	50	55	53
Can't/won't choose	15	14	14
N (minimum)	6,362	13,959	20,321

Source: SNP internal survey of party members

The referendum did bring a slightly more working-class support to the party but only very slightly: 65 per cent even of
the newer recruits are in classes A and B, while only 13 per
cent were in the manual working classes D and E. This leaves
a membership that, like that of other parties, is dominated
by the modern professions. Clearly a lot of those objectively
middle-class people nonetheless identify as working class,
given that this is the subjective identity of more than half of
the membership. This reinforces the point made earlier in this
book about the associations between working-class, left-wing
and Scottish identity. But these associations were not forged
by the referendum and so with subjective identity, too, there
has been only a small shift in the working-class direction.

There are more noticeable changes when it comes to age
and gender. The average age of members has fallen from
fifty-five to fifty-one as a result of post-referendum recruitment, and the oldest and youngest age groups are now
roughly equal in size compared to the 3:1 ratio among pre-
referendum members. Again, however, the point should not
be overstated: 54 per cent of those new recruits were over
fifty and the age profile of the SNP's membership, like that
of other parties, could still be mistaken for that of a golf
club. Most of the more youthful 'Yes' supporters channelled
their post-referendum zeal into less middle-aged activities.
Meanwhile, the near-gender parity among new recruits is
striking for two reasons. First, across parties it is typical for
membership to be at least 60 per cent male (Bale and Webb,

2015) and so this new SNP cohort is unusually female at least in relative terms. Second, this was achieved on the back of campaigning for a policy disproportionately popular among males. Other things remaining the same, then, we would not have expected the surge generated by an independence referendum to boost the SNP's recruitment of female members. One other thing that conspicuously did not remain the same, of course, was the party's leader. And, while here we are inevitably speculating beyond the data in Table 8.2, it is hard to believe that that succession – and the amount of attention paid to Nicola Sturgeon, often emphasising her sex as the one undeniable difference with her predecessor – did not play a significant part in bringing more women into the party.

The big expansion in the SNP vote between 2007 and 2011 had little effect on the profile of the party's electorate. SNP voters had not changed much; there were just more of them. The same can be said of the membership between 2014 and 2015 – except that in this case there are a *lot* more of them. This reflects the extraordinary mobilising capacity of the referendum in general and the 'Yes' campaign in particular. Nevertheless, while that did bring into the SNP some of the kinds of citizens who have not typically been attracted to party membership in recent times, it brought in far more of exactly the kinds of people who were always attracted to party membership. This rather conventional option for pursuing the cause of independence was chosen by a rather conventional-looking subset of 'Yes' supporters.

This still leaves open the possibility that the new recruits are distinct in attitudes and priorities. We saw in Chapter 3 that the average voter continues to perceive the SNP as just to the left of centre and the same was true of party members when asked about the party in 2007: on average, the members placed both the party and themselves at around 4.5 on a scale from 0 (left) to 10 (right). These perceptions would probably please the leadership of a party that has long sought to present itself as a moderate left-of-centre party (Mitchell, 1996, p. 232). But the arguments and rhetoric of the 'Yes' campaign sounded appreciably to the left of that, and so the same might

FIGURE 8.2: AVERAGE LEFT–RIGHT SELF-PLACEMENTS OF EXISTING
AND NEW SNP MEMBERS AND VOTERS

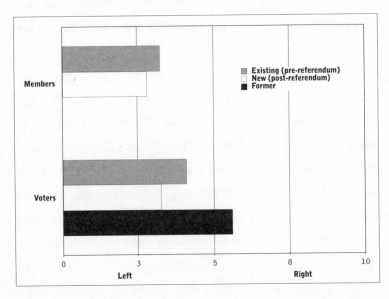

Sources: British Party Members survey (Bale and Webb, 2015); Scottish Referendum
Study 2014; British Election Study Internet Panel Wave 6.

well be true of the members that it brought into the SNP. The first pair of bars in Figure 8.2 confirms this leftward shift in the party's grassroots. Those recruited after the referendum do indeed see themselves as rather more left-wing than those already in the party. If the difference is not very large, this is partly because some more left-leaning members had already been attracted to the party during the referendum campaign itself. Both results in Figure 8.2 mark a pronounced leftward shift compared with that 2007 figure mentioned above.

The same is true of the party's electorate. New voters, defined as those who voted SNP in 2015 but not in 2011, are discernibly more left-wing than those who chose the SNP in both elections. The voters, old and new, remain more moderate than the party members. Nonetheless, the clear picture is of a party base whose ideological centre of gravity has shifted to the left.

An important caveat is necessary here. Left-wing identity is not the same as left-wing policy preferences. This has been highlighted in recent comparisons of the Scottish and English electorates (e.g. Henderson, 2014), which reveal minimal differences on policy issues but more marked differences in left–right self-placement. Put crudely, the Scots are not more left-wing than the English, but they think they are – perhaps understandably, given their mass rejection of right-wing parties. It is not hard to imagine that, if independence became seen partly as a means of protecting left-wing Scotland from right-wing England, those in the party of

independence would become increasingly unlikely to identify as anything other than left-wing. This does not mean that
they will demand or even necessarily prefer left-wing policies, however. That is a crucial point because the SNP would
be granted a lot more leeway in office from a membership
that only identifies as left-wing than from one with a clearly
left-wing policy agenda.

The fact that the SNP's members and voters might not be
as left-wing as they seem is one reason to doubt comparisons
with radical left parties like Podemos and Syriza that have
made similarly spectacular electoral gains, and comparisons
with the intra-party shifts to the left that propelled Jeremy
Corbyn and Bernie Sanders into public attention. There are
two other reasons why these comparisons are exaggerated.
First, the SNP is not a new, radical, grassroots force. In this
respect, it was the 'Yes' campaign that more closely resem-
bled Podemos or the Five Star Movement in Italy. The SNP
is a conventional political party with an existing and com-
paratively moderate support base. Second, it is also a party
that was already in a dominant electoral position before the
referendum. Hence, while the party gained many members
and voters from that same tide that has lifted left-wing boats
elsewhere, it also had something to lose.

The strategic dilemma faced by the party's leadership is
highlighted by the darker bar in Figure 8.2. It shows the
average left–right position of *former* SNP voters – those who
voted SNP in 2011 but not in 2015 – and thus illustrates the

electoral cost of being seen to move to the left. The aim of a 'catch-all' party is always to expand rather than to move. If the SNP could attract those who would elsewhere vote for Syriza or Jeremy Corbyn then it had no intention of turning them away, but it had no wish to lose any existing support in the process. But being truly 'catch-all' is more a matter of aspiration than achievement. Expansion in one ideological direction almost inevitably means contraction on the other side, and success is measured in the relative size of those gains and losses. The SNP was successful in 2015 because, in the terms of Figure 8.2, 14 per cent of the Scottish electorate were 'new voters' and only 9 per cent were 'former voters'. Continued success depends on maintaining that ratio and, hence, on the delicate task of combining a radical appeal with a reputation for moderation.

'IF WE WANT THINGS TO CHANGE, THINGS WILL HAVE TO STAY AS THEY ARE'

Nicola Sturgeon was immediately charged with that task. She came to the leadership with a reputation for leaning more to the left than her predecessor. This impression was shared by voters, according to a September 2015 YouGov poll. Sturgeon was deemed to be either 'very' or 'fairly' left-wing by 44 per cent of respondents, compared to 37 per cent for Salmond. Profiles of the new leader made much of her council house background in Irvine and the instinctive sympathy to working-class interests that it was held to have given her. Insofar as all this made Sturgeon seem more in tune with the radical mood of the 'Yes' campaign, it will only have helped the party's post-referendum expansion. In truth, though, the change of leader brought no change of direction. Sturgeon and Salmond have much in common. Both come from respectable working-class small-town backgrounds. Both in the past have called themselves socialists but now prefer social democrat. And the two had worked too closely together to suggest anything but continuity after the succession. Sturgeon was a leader-in-waiting but not one awaiting the opportunity to radically overhaul strategy or to lurch to the left. Nor did the election of her deputy suggest a new direction or a radical new membership. Stewart Hosie, SNP MP for Dundee East, defeated Keith Brown and Angela Constance, both MSPs, in the second round of voting. Hosie had been a loyal supporter of the leadership, especially John Swinney, and gave no impression that he sought a change of strategy – though neither did the others to any significant extent.

The policy direction of the SNP government was also little affected. Sturgeon as First Minister did place increased emphasis on community engagement in the development of public policy, seeking to harness the energy and enthusiasm evident in the referendum campaign. However, central government initiatives and new laws to facilitate participation can sit uneasily with grassroots participation and community empowerment. On coming to power, the SNP had removed many of the detailed controls that central government wields over local authorities, but frustration with the pace of change inclined it to revert to a more controlling approach, as is common when a party has served two terms. There is little evidence that the new leadership is about to allow a thousand flowers to bloom, as the SNP did by necessity during the referendum when it encouraged the creation and activities of a range of groups arguing for independence, or to permit candidates with limited background in the party to contest elections under its banner – at least, not without much stricter scrutiny of applications than there was in 2015. With two of its new MPs, Michelle Thomson and Natalie McGarry, suspended from the party within just six months of the 2015 election, the party saw grounds for re-establishing tighter control. The SNP's election campaigns and governing styles are returning to the highly professional, centrally controlled, evidence-based, focus group-tested, risk-averse approach that emerged over the course of devolution. This is likely to mean the same moderation and 'catch-all' approach that was successful in 2011.

The question then becomes one about how a leadership committed to moderation can manage the ambitions and expectations of those new members and voters who seek a more radical approach. First, this is not a new challenge for the SNP – it amounts to the same fundamentalist/pragmatist tensions that were documented in Chapter 6, although there is now also the need to balance a reputation for moderation and governing competence alongside claims to be radical and anti-austerity. Second, these (like any other) tensions are greatly eased by electoral success. This is not simply because of a general mood-lifting effect; it is also because both fundamentalists and pragmatists within the SNP would agree that independence is more likely when the party is in power. Our survey of SNP members in late 2007, six months into the party's first ever term of national office, revealed an almost Panglossian view of party strategy, including the simultaneous agreement with both fundamentalist and pragmatist statements. It is a lot easier to agree – as did 81 per cent of members in that survey – that 'the SNP should always stand by its principles even if this loses votes' when those votes are already in the bag.

The same unifying effect of success was felt throughout the run-up to and euphoric aftermath of the 2015 election. It also helped a lot that this was a UK general election, encouraging the SNP to use the kind of anti-austerity, anti-Westminster-establishment messages – in effect, all the premises of the 'Yes' campaign but this time stopping short of its conclusion of independence – that would appeal most to its new recruits. It would have been harder in 2015, and will be harder in 2016, to please these more uncompromising members and voters with the kind of 'safe pair of hands' campaign that the party has run for Holyrood elections. Instead, 2015 offered the ideal combination: the SNP could project a radical image without any risk of having to act upon it in office.

If the same rhetoric brings the SNP a majority in 2016, the party will then be under pressure to use that majority not just to mount an anti-austerity programme of government but also in pursuit of independence.

Both elections are nonetheless an invaluable means for the SNP of refocusing support for 'Yes' onto the party. Rather than reflecting on the past referendum and agitating for another, the more energetic SNP activists have been distracted by two national elections within two years of the referendum. Meanwhile, the less energetic place little strain on party unity. And there are plenty of these armchair members. The survey in late 2015 asked members whether they had attended any of a number of SNP- or 'Yes'-related meetings and events, and 55 per cent of post-referendum recruits had attended none. This compares to just 39 per cent of those who had joined the party at some point before the referendum. So, while the participatory zeal of 2014 has by no means waned completely, there was bound to be a slow shift back in that direction – the SNP neither expected nor needed the extraordinary atmosphere of the referendum and its aftermath to persist. At the same time, not long enough has passed since the referendum for the party's supporters to have worked up uncontrollable impatience about a re-run. In a Survation poll conducted a year after the September 2014 vote, only one in three of those who had voted SNP in 2015 felt that there should be another referendum within two years. This is not a trivial proportion but it suggests that the party line – to avoid any talk of timing and to refer only to 'material change in circumstances' – is largely holding.

But perhaps the most important reason why the SNP is able to retain support from its more radical wing while maintaining a pragmatic or moderate line is that there is no significant threat coming up on its radical outside. There is another echo of New Labour here, although in that case the protection came via a majoritarian electoral system which meant that declining enthusiasm and vote shares in the party's heartlands did not cost it any seats. The Scottish party system is more open than that and the SNP has experience from the 2003 Holyrood elections of losing votes to more radical left parties. When it comes to independence, however, there is no meaningful threat on the fundamentalist side that obliges the SNP to tack in that direction. And, crucially, independence is the decisive issue for these new recruits. Another question from that recent membership survey asked respondents to choose among a list of reasons which best describes why they joined the SNP. It is not surprising that fully 75 per cent chose 'I want to see Scotland become independent'. More noteworthy is that that percentage was virtually identical (74 per cent) among the newest recruits. Those post-referendum joiners were slightly more likely than longer-standing members to cite 'to work for a more equal society' and 'I lost faith in the Labour Party', in line with the more left-wing stance shown in Figure 8.2. But their overall responses point to independence remaining the top priority.

Of course, some party members will have seen this question as presenting a false choice. Independence is seen by many as a means to those more left-wing ends. Indeed, the success of the 'Yes' campaign from an SNP standpoint was exactly to forge a tighter link between independence and goals like equality and social justice – goals central to the way in which Scottish political identity has been distinguished from English political identity. The stronger that link, the more the SNP establishes its own left-wing credentials simply through its support for independence, even if its policy offerings elsewhere tend to the mildly social democratic.

All of this goes a long way to insulating the SNP against rival parties like the Greens and against new forces like RISE (Respect, Independence, Socialism and Environmentalism), the left-wing alliance born out of some of the more radical strands of the referendum campaign. In different ways, both have characteristics that might appeal to those who joined the SNP after the referendum and voted for the party in 2015. They are more radical in left–right terms and more grassroots-driven than the SNP, and are also less constrained in terms of the urgency with which they can demand independence. However, at least for the foreseeable future, neither – especially RISE, whose media profile dwarfs its poll rating – will come anywhere near the electorally dominant SNP on the key question: which of these options offers the more plausible route to independence? Those for whom 'I' – as opposed to 'R', 'S' or 'E' – remains the top priority are likely to stick with the SNP.

After the referendum, many independence supporters proudly sported badges with '45' to emphasise how far they had come. They thereby reminded the SNP that an electoral majority is hard to build on support for independence alone. The party will therefore continue to pursue what might be called 'don't rock the boat' politics at Holyrood, knowing both that this can attract 'No' voters and that most convinced 'Yes' supporters will see no viable alternative route to independence. The dual political arenas in a devolved Scotland, in which the SNP can project a radical and anti-establishment image in a UK context but appear as a safe pair of governing hands at home, make it much easier for the party to satisfy multiple audiences. Until now, at least, the SNP has been extraordinarily successful in being both a party of protest and a party of power.

LOOKING AHEAD

It is an understatement to say that the SNP's current electoral supremacy was not widely foreseen. Hindsight, however, enables us to assess whether it might have been predictable. To answer that question, it is useful to borrow the sociologists' distinction between structure and agency: that is, between the institutions or other rules and norms that constrain political parties on the one hand, and those actors' decisions and behaviour on the other. Devolution was the key structural change and was probably a necessary condition for the SNP's soaring vote shares. It created an arena in which the SNP was strategically or 'mathematically' viable, and in which Labour was pitted against an opponent much harder to beat than were the Conservatives on the crucial 'Scottish interests' dimension. However, devolution alone was not a sufficient condition. The SNP made choices in terms of its organisation, its leadership, its campaigning style, and its approach to government that maximised the devolution dividend. And then, of course, there is luck. The SNP won in 2007 by little more than a hair's breadth. In 2011, it won the majority that enabled the independence referendum on a 45 per cent vote – slightly less on the regional list – and hence thanks to the disproportional vagaries of the electoral system. Had either of those election results been only slightly different, this book would have been very different – if it had been written at all.

What does this imply for the future? That necessary condition of devolution seems set to remain in place. It is therefore hard to imagine any scenario in the foreseeable future in which the SNP is not at least a viable contender for office at Holyrood. However, there is a distinction between being in contention to lead a coalition and being in contention for a majority. Maintaining the latter status requires the SNP to do one of two things. The first is to retain the major valence advantages – in terms of perceived competence, leadership and party image – that it has since 2011 enjoyed over all of its rivals. This seems to be in the bag for 2016 but is far from guaranteed thereafter. As the experience of New Labour shows, there is something easy-come, easy-go about valence success. If a party chooses the wrong leader or loses its reputation for competence, the votes can drain away as quickly as they poured in. We noted in Chapter 5 that the SNP's overall ratings were rather better than evaluations of their performance on specific issues like health and education. If disquiet about the latter grows, there may be a tipping point at which the general reputation for competence is undermined too.

If that valence approach is what delivered the 45 per cent in 2011, the second route to a majority is to capture the rather different 45 per cent who voted 'Yes' in the referendum. This chapter has shown that it was the latter who stuck with the SNP in the general election of 2015. The question for 2016, then, is whether there will be a return to 'normal service' at Holyrood elections or whether the referendum triggered a more permanent electoral realignment – perhaps even one in which the SNP performs worse in a Holyrood election than the preceding Westminster vote. The analysis in the previous chapter suggested the second result: that the SNP's virtual monopoly over supporters of independence in 2016 will offset its losses among 2011 SNP voters for whom a 'No' vote was a gateway out of the party. If so, then the recipe for continued electoral success is rather different. It depends on support for independence remaining around or above its referendum level, and on the SNP maintaining that monopoly over this group – which may in turn require at least a nod in the more fundamentalist direction.

More than one audience will be looking out for such a nod in the party's 2016 manifesto (which was yet to be published at the time of writing). Gone are the days in which mention of a referendum was seen as a gradualist dilution; now commitment will be measured – at least by some in the broader independence movement – by the prominence and imminence of a referendum. Nicola Sturgeon has already said that the manifesto 'will set out what we consider are the circumstances and the timescale on which a second referendum might be appropriate' (BBC, 2015) but the devil will be in the detail – or lack thereof. If the post-referendum SNP is sticking to anything like the pragmatic line that proved successful in pre-referendum Holyrood elections, there will be few particulars.

One specific scenario that probably has to be addressed, given that the EU membership referendum is within weeks of the Holyrood election, is the possibility of 'Brexit' despite what looks likely to be a clear Scottish majority for remaining in. Although this is generally portrayed as a great opportunity for the SNP, it may actually present a major headache. Sturgeon has acknowledged that such a scenario would 'almost certainly' feed demands for a second independence referendum. That was then widely misreported as her saying that it would 'almost certainly' trigger another referendum. Certainly it would place the SNP leader under intense pressure from within her party. If Brexit did not constitute a 'material change in circumstances', then many members and possibly some of Sturgeon's colleagues would wonder aloud what would.

In fact, the 'material change' that the SNP is really looking for is a consistent and clear polling majority for independence. It is quite likely that, if Scotland votes for 'Bremain' but is outvoted by the rest of the UK, this hard evidence of diverging opinion is likely to boost independence support in the polls. However, that boost might be quite small and quite fleeting. It is small even in hypothetical polling questions. In February 2016, an Ipsos MORI poll asked respondents to 'imagine the UK as a whole votes to leave the EU in the referendum when voters in Scotland vote to remain in the EU. If this led to another Scottish independence referendum being held, how would you vote?' Support for independence was only five percentage points higher (54 per cent rather than 49 per cent) than in a straight referendum question with no 'Brexit' preamble. Since such clumsy hypotheticals (another example being the ubiquitous 'would you be more likely to vote for party X if it changed its leader?' question) are notorious for exaggerating the likely impact of each change, this five-point difference is actually strikingly small, not strikingly large.

The reason is not hard to find. Those voters likely to be most inflamed by Scotland being dragged out of the EU by the rest of the UK are already in the 'Yes' camp. Moreover, in many cases this ire might have more to do with the imposition of UK political will on a dissenting Scotland than with any particular concern over the European issue.

In the independence referendum, expectations about either Scotland's or the UK's membership of the EU were not very influential over voting choices – much less so than expectations about the economy, inequality and further devolution. So we should not overestimate the wider Scottish public's outrage in the event of the Scots being overruled in a UK-wide 'Leave' vote in June. Then there is the possibility that 'Brexit' would make a second independence referendum harder for the SNP to win. Questions about the currency and EU accession would become different but no easier to answer, and then be supplemented by all the questions arising from Scotland's main trading partner being outside the EU. That surge in support for independence following 'Brexit' might ebb once its implications sink in.

Nicola Sturgeon and the SNP's words have been chosen carefully. While 'material change' is the official line, behind this lies an even more significant unspoken consideration. The SNP cannot afford to lose a second referendum. It emerged from the 2014 defeat stronger because the result was much better than expectations had been at the outset, and because of the mobilising energy that the party could harness. But a second referendum is likely to be very different, especially if held sooner than later. The mood among supporters of independence would be very different in the event of a second defeat. Expectations of victory will have been far greater. And there would be only the remotest prospect of a third referendum in the foreseeable future. Any post-referendum energy is likely to be negative and to turn against the party leadership – indeed, it is hard to see how the leader could avoid resignation – and internal recriminations and feuding seem likely. We dwelt on 1979 in Chapter 6 because of the long-term damage that that experience wrought on the SNP. A second referendum defeat in the short to medium term would be another 1979 – or worse.

It is therefore difficult to see the 2016 election result having a rapid or direct bearing on Scotland's constitutional future. Unless there is a major late swing against the SNP – and notably one that leaves it reliant on small coalition partners with a more radical stance on independence – then the party will get its majority but will not necessarily want to use it for the pursuit of independence. The difficulty lies not in making the case that there has been material change but in convincing a clear majority of Scottish voters over a sustained period to support independence – while convincing party members and the wider independence movement to wait that long. That clear majority does not currently exist and we can only speculate about the circumstances likely to generate it. Perhaps the most plausible scenario at the moment is a referendum on independence held on the basis of an SNP Holyrood manifesto commitment in 2021 after the return of another Conservative government at Westminster a year earlier. But that is many weeks away, each of which is potentially a long time in politics. The SNP's ultimate goal, tantalisingly close in September 2014, may yet prove very distant.

REFERENCES

Andersen, R. and Evans, G., 2003. 'Who Blairs wins? Leadership and voting in the 2001 election', *British Elections & Parties Yearbook*, 13(1), 229–47.

Ashcroft, M. and Culwick, K., 2015. *Pay Me Forty Quid and I'll Tell You*, London: Biteback.

Bale, T. and Webb, P., 2015. 'Grunts in the Ground Game: UK Party Members in the 2015 General Election', paper prepared for the conference on 'The 2015 British General Election: Parties, Politics, and the Future of the United Kingdom', 2 September 2015, Berkeley, CA.

Bartle, J. and Crewe, I., 2002. 'The impact of party leaders in Britain: Strong assumptions, weak evidence', in King, A. (ed.), *Leaders' Personalities and the Outcomes of Democratic Elections*, Oxford: Oxford University Press.

BBC, 2004. 'Salmond launches leadership bid', Scotland Politics, 15 July, available at http://news.bbc.co.uk/1/hi/scotland/3895575.stm.

BBC, 2015. 'SNP manifesto to reveal possible second referendum timetable', Scotland Politics, 13 September, available at http://www.bbc.co.uk/news/uk-scotland-scotland-politics-34234024.

Beller, D. and Belloni, F., 1978. 'The study of factions' in Belloni, F. and Beller, D. (eds), *Faction Politics: Political Parties and Factionalism in Comparative Perspective*, Santa Barbara, CA: ABC-Clio.

Bennie, L., Brand, J., and Mitchell, J., 1997. *How Scotland Votes*. Manchester: Manchester University Press.

Blain, N., Hutchison, D. and Hassan, G. (eds), 2016. *Scotland's Referendum and the Media*, Edinburgh: Edinburgh University Press.

Bochel, J. M. and Denver, D., 1981. 'The outcome', in Bochel, J. M. (ed.), *The Referendum Experience: Scotland 1979*, Oxford: Pergamon.

Brand, J., 1978. *The National Movement in Scotland*, London: Routledge.

British Election Study, 2015. 'Learning the right lessons from Labour's 2015 defeat', available at http://www.britishelectionstudy.com/ bes-impact/learning-the-right-lessons-from-labours-2015-defeat/#. Vr8UA_mLTcs.

Brown, A., McCrone, D., Paterson, L. and Surridge, P., 1999. *The Scottish Electorate: The 1997 General Elections and Beyond*, Basingstoke: Macmillan.

Bryant, C., 2014. *Parliament: The Biography, Volume II: Reform*, London: Doubleday.

Budge, I. and Urwin, D. W., 1966. *Scottish Political Behaviour: A Case Study in British Homogeneity, Volume 3*, London: Longmans Green.

Butt, S., 2006. 'How voters evaluate economic competence: A comparison between parties in and out of power', *Political Studies*, 54(4), 743–66.

Carman, C., Johns, R. and Mitchell, J., 2014. *More Scottish than British: The 2011 Scottish Parliament Election*, Basingstoke: Palgrave Macmillan.

Carman, C., Mitchell, J. and Johns, R., 2008. 'The unfortunate natural experiment in ballot design: the Scottish Parliamentary Elections of 2007', *Electoral Studies*, 27(3), 442–59.

Clarke, H., Sanders, D., Stewart, M. and Whiteley, P., 2004. *Political Choice in Britain*, Oxford: Oxford University Press.

Clarke, H., Sanders, D., Stewart, M. and Whiteley, P., 2009. *Performance Politics and the British Voter*, Cambridge: Cambridge University Press.

Constitution Unit, 2003. 'Nations and Regions: The Dynamics of Devolution', Quarterly Monitoring Programme, Scotland, Quarterly Report, November 2003. Available at https://www.ucl.ac.uk/constitution-unit/research/research-archive/dmr99-04/scotland_november_2003.pdf.

Convery, A., 2014. 'The 2011 Scottish Conservative Party Leadership Election: Dilemmas for Statewide Parties in Regional Contexts', *Parliamentary Affairs*, 67(2).

Curtice, J., 2006. 'Is Holyrood accountable and representative?', in Bromley, C., Curtice, J., McCrone, D. and Park, A. (eds), *Has Devolution Delivered?*, Edinburgh: Edinburgh University Press, 90–108.

Curtice, J., McCrone, D., McEwen, N., Marsh, M. and Ormston, R., 2009. *Revolution or Evolution? The 2007 Scottish Elections*, Edinburgh: Edinburgh University Press.

Dahlgreen, W., 2015. 'YouGov Profiles: Nicola Sturgeon is Scotland's most popular person', available at https://yougov.co.uk/news/2015/11/01/nicola-sturgeon-scotlands-most-popular-person.

Daily Record, 2016. '"Get the Pakis out of the party": SNP councillor Julie McAnulty at the centre of second race row', News, 8 February, available at http://www.dailyrecord.co.uk/news/politics/get-pakis-out-party-snp-7328646.

Davies, R., 1999. 'Devolution – A Process, Not an Event', Cardiff: Institute of Welsh Affairs.

Denver, D., 2015. 'The Results: How Britain Voted', *Parliamentary Affairs*, 68(suppl. 1), 5–24.

Denver, D. T., Pattie, C., Mitchell, J., Bochel, H., 2000. *Scotland Decides: The Devolution Issue and the 1997 Referendum*, London, Frank Cass.

Devine, T., 2013. 'Remarkable change in standing of Catholics', *Herald Scotland*, 9 January, available at http://www.heraldscotland.com/opinion/13087488.Remarkable_change_in_standing_of_Catholics.

Dewar Gibb., A., 1930. *Scotland in Eclipse*, London: H. Toulmin.

Drucker, H. M., 1978. *Breakaway: The Scottish Labour Party*, Edinburgh: Edinburgh University Students' Publication Board.

Edinburgh Evening News, 2014. 'Tommy Sheppard won't rule out standing for SNP', 25 September, available at http://www.edinburghnews.scotsman.com/news/tommy-sheppard-won-t-rule-out-standing-for-snp-1-3552636#ixzz403Wp7Dav.

Evans, G. and Andersen, R., 2005. 'The impact of party leaders: How Blair lost Labour votes', *Parliamentary Affairs*, 58(4), 818–36.

Evans, G. and Tilley, J., 2012. 'How parties shape class politics: Explaining the decline of the class basis of party support', *British Journal of Political Science*, 42(1), 137–61.

Finlay, R., 1994. *Independent and Free: Scottish Politics and the Origins of the Scottish National Party 1918–1945*, Edinburgh: John Donald.

Ford, R. and Goodwin, M., 2014. *Revolt on the Right: Explaining Support for the Radical Right in Britain*, London: Routledge.

Gardham, M., 2014. 'Salmond: "I'm Scottish … and British"', *Herald Scotland*, 17 January, available at http://www.heraldscotland.com/news/13140940.Salmond__I_m_Scottish___and_British.

Geoghegan, P., 2014. *The People's Referendum: Why Scotland Will Never Be the Same Again.* Edinburgh: Luath Press.

Goldhill, O., 2014. 'Alex Salmond's "female problem" – or why most Scottish women wouldn't trust him to run a tea party', *Daily Telegraph*, 11 September, available at http://www.telegraph.co.uk/news/uknews/scotland/11090459/Alex-Salmonds-female-problem-or-why-most-Scottish-women-wouldnt-trust-him-to-run-a-tea-party.html.

Gould, R., 2007. 'Independent review of the Scottish parliamentary and local government elections 3 May 2007', Edinburgh: Electoral Commission.

Green-Pedersen, C., 2001. 'Minority governments and party politics: the political and institutional background to the "Danish miracle"', *Journal of Public Policy*, 21(1), 53–70.

Griesbach, D., Robertson, L., Waterton, J. and Birch, A., 2012. 'Your Scotland, Your Referendum: An Analysis of Consultation Responses', Edinburgh: Scottish Government Social Research.

Guardian, 2010. 'Scottish government "shocked" by Megrahi outcry', US embassy cables: the documents, 7 December, available at http://www.theguardian.com/world/us-embassy-cables-documents/222002.

Hassan, G. and Shaw, E., 2012. *The Strange Death of Labour Scotland*, Edinburgh: Edinburgh University Press.

Henderson, A., 2014. 'The myth of a meritocratic Scotland', in Cowley, P. and Ford, R. (eds), *Sex, Lies and the Ballot Box*, London: Biteback.

Herald, 1998. 'Winning praises nationalist rebirth: Cardinal sees future in Europe', News, 5 October, available at http://www.heraldscotland.com/news/12336000.Winning_praises_nationalist_rebirth_Cardinal_sees_future_in_Europe.

Herald, 2013. 'Galloway attacked for SNP Catholic slur', News, 19 May, available at http://www.heraldscotland.com/news/13105420.Galloway_attacked_for_SNP_Catholic_slur.

Herald, 2014. 'SNP membership trebles following indyref', News, 1 October, available at http://www.heraldscotland.com/news/13182725.SNP_membership_trebles_following_indyref.

Herald, 2015. 'J. K. Rowling: "There's still anti-English prejudice in the SNP"', News, 18 June. Available at http://www.heraldscotland.com/news/13413390.JK_Rowling__there_s_still_anti_English_prejudice_in_the_SNP.

Hobolt, S. B., 2007. 'Taking cues on Europe? Voter competence and party endorsements in referendums on European integration', *European Journal of Political Research*, 46(2), 151–82.

Hunt, T., 2012. 'Olympic opening ceremony: Tristram Hunt's review', *The Guardian*, 28 July, available at http://www.theguardian.com/sport/2012/jul/28/olympics-opening-ceremony-tristram-hunt-review.

Hussain, A. and Miller, W., 2006. *Multicultural Nationalism: Islamophobia, Anglophobia, and Devolution*, Oxford: Oxford University Press.

Johns, R. A., Mitchell, J., Denver, D. and Pattie, C., 2010. *Voting for a Scottish Government: The Scottish Parliament Election of 2007*, Manchester: Manchester University Press.

Johns, R., Bennie, L. and Mitchell, J., 2012. 'Gendered nationalism: The gender gap in support for the Scottish National Party', *Party Politics*, 18(4), 581–601.

Keating, M., 1988. *State and Regional Nationalism: Territorial Politics and the European State*, London: Harvester Wheatsheaf.

Kellas, J., 1998. *The Politics of Nationalism and Ethnicity* (2nd edn), Basingstoke: Palgrave Macmillan.

Kerevan, G., 1991. 'Labourism Revisited', in *Chapman*, vol.35–36, 25–31.

King, A., 2002. *Leaders' Personalities and the Outcomes of Democratic Elections*, Oxford: Oxford University Press.

Kriesi, H., 2005. *Direct Democratic Choice: The Swiss Experience*, Lanham, MD: Lexington Books.

Lau, R. R. and Redlawsk, D. P., 2001. 'Advantages and disadvantages of cognitive heuristics in political decision making', *American Journal of Political Science*, 45(4), 951–71.

Lau, R. R., Sigelman, L. and Rovner, I. B., 2007. 'The effects of negative political campaigns: a meta-analytic reassessment', *Journal of Politics*, 69(4), 1176–1209.

Lloyd, M., 2007. 'Uncharted waters', *Inside Housing*, 25 May, 19–20.

Lodge, M. and Taber, C. S., 2000. 'Three steps toward a theory of motivated political reasoning', in Lupia, A., McCubbins, M. and Popkin, S. (eds), *Elements of Reason: Cognition, Choice, and the Bounds of Rationality*, London: Cambridge University Press, 183–213.

Macartney, A., 1981. 'The Protagonists', in Bochel, J. M. (ed.), *The Referendum Experience: Scotland 1979*, Oxford: Pergamon Press.

Macartney, A. and Brown, A., 1990. 'Independence in Europe', in *Scottish Government Yearbook 1990*, Edinburgh: Unit for the Study of Government in Scotland.

MacAskill, K., 2004. 'Time for a Convention on Fiscal Autonomy', *Holyrood Magazine*, April 2014.

McCrone, D., 1992. *Understanding Scotland: The Sociology of a Stateless Nation*, London: Routledge.

McCrone, D., 2001. *Understanding Scotland: The Sociology of a Nation*, London: Routledge.

MacDonald, D. (@DJMacDSTV), 2014. Twitter post: 'Edinburgh Uni Prof James Mitchell post #indyref verdict – "The losing side are behaving like the winners and the winners acting like losers"', 23 September, URL: https://twitter.com/DJMacDSTV/status/514355399861215232.

McIntosh, I., Sim, D. and Robertson, D., 2004. '"It's as if you're some alien...": Exploring anti-English attitudes in Scotland', *Sociological Research Online*, 9(2).

Macwhirter, I., 2014. *Disunited Kingdom: How Westminster Won a Referendum but Lost Scotland*, Glasgow: Cargo.

Marcus, G. E., Neuman, W. R. and MacKuen, M., 2000. *Affective Intelligence and Political Judgment*, Chicago: University of Chicago Press.

Maxwell, S., 2013. *The Case for Left Wing Nationalism*. Edinburgh: Luath Press.

May, J. D., 1973. 'Opinion structure of political parties: The special law of curvilinear disparity', *Political Studies*, 21(2), 135–51.

Miller, W. L., 1981. *The End of British Politics?*, Oxford: Clarendon.

Mills, R., 2010. 'Man behind racist Scots group named', *Sunday Express*, 11 January, available at http://www.express.co.uk/news/uk/151081/Man-behind-racist-Scots-group-named.

Mitchell, J., 1996. *Strategies for Self-Government: The Campaigns for a Scottish Parliament*, Edinburgh: Polygon.

Mitchell, J., 1998. 'The evolution of devolution: Labour's home rule strategy in opposition', *Government and Opposition*, 33(4), 479–96.

Mitchell, J., Bennie, L. and Johns, R., 2012. *The Scottish National Party: Transition to Power*, Oxford: Oxford University Press.

Morrison, J., 2015. 'The "RISE" of the Scottish left is challenging the SNP's hegemony in Scotland', Democratic Audit Scotland, 19 October, available at http://www.democraticauditscotland.com/the-rise-of-the-scottish-left-challenging-snp-hegemony-in-scotland.

Mughan, A., 2000. *Media and the Presidentialization of Parliamentary Elections*, New York: Palgrave.

National Archives, 1979. Note of telephone conversation between the PM and the Lord President at 4.20 p.m., 2 March, London: National Archives of the UK.

Naurin, E., 2011. *Election Promises, Party Behaviour and Voter Perceptions*, Basingstoke: Palgrave Macmillan.

Ormston, R., 2013. 'Why don't more women support independence? Findings from the Scottish Social Attitudes survey', Edinburgh: ScotCen, available at http://www.scotcen.org.uk/media/176043/gender-and-indep-paper-final-2012.pdf.

Park, A. and McCrone, D., 2006. 'The devolution conundrum?' in Bromley, C., Curtice, J., McCrone, D. and Park, A. (eds), *Has Devolution Delivered?*, Edinburgh: Edinburgh University Press, 15–28.

Paterson, L. 2006. 'Sources of support for the SNP', in Bromley, C., Curtice, J., McCrone, D. and Park, A. (eds), *Has Devolution Delivered?*, Edinburgh: Edinburgh University Press, 46–68.

Paterson, L., Brown, A., Curtice, J., Hinds, K., McCrone, D., Park, A., Sproston, K. and Surridge, P., 2001. *New Scotland, New Politics?*, Edinburgh: Polygon.

Pattie, C., Denver, D., Johns, R. and Mitchell, J., 2011. 'Raising the tone? The impact of "positive" and "negative" campaigning on voting in the 2007 Scottish Parliament election', *Electoral Studies*, 30(2), 333–43.

Pattie, C. and Johnston, R., 2000. '"People who talk together vote together": An exploration of contextual effects in Great Britain', *Annals of the Association of American Geographers*, 90(1), 41–66.

Peace, T. and Meer, N., 2015. 'The 2015 Election: BME Groups in Scotland', in Khan, O., Sveinsson, K. (eds), *Race and Elections*, London: Runnymede Perspectives.

Pike, J., 2015. *Project Fear: How an Unlikely Alliance Left a Kingdom United but a Country Divided*, London: Biteback.

Pulzer, P. G. J., 1967. *Political Representation and Elections: Parties and Voting in Great Britain*, New York: Praeger.

Renwick, A., 2014. 'Don't trust your poll lead: How public opinion changes during referendum campaigns', in Cowley, P. and Ford, R. (eds), *Sex, Lies and the Ballot Box*, London: Biteback.

Ritchie, M., 2000. *Scotland Reclaimed: The Inside Story of Scotland's First Democratic Parliamentary Election*, Edinburgh: The Saltire Society.

Salmond, A., 2008. Cardinal Winning Education Lecture, 2 February, Glasgow, available at http://www.gov.scot/News/Speeches/Speeches/First-Minister/cardwinlecture.

Scotsman, 2011. '"Stern Nicola Sturgeon keeps me in check" – Alex Salmond', News, 10 June, available at http://www.scotsman.com/news/stern-nicola-sturgeon-keeps-me-in-check-alex-salmond-1-1680795.

Scottish Executive, 2007. 'Choosing Scotland's Future: A National Conversation', Edinburgh: Scottish Executive, available at http://www.gov.scot/Resource/Doc/194791/0052321.pdf.

Scottish Government, 2010. 'Your Scotland, Your Voice', White Paper, November 2009, http://www.scotland.gov.uk/Publications/2009/11/26155932/0.

Scottish Government. 2011. 'Summary: Ethnic Group Demographics', available at http://www.gov.scot/Topics/People/Equality/Equalities/DataGrid/Ethnicity/EthPopMig.

Scottish Government, 2012. 'Your Scotland, Your Referendum', Consultation, January, https://consult.scotland.gov.uk/elections-and-constitutional-development-division/scotreferendum-external/supporting_documents/00386122.pdf.

Scottish Government, 2013. 'Scotland's Future: Your Guide to an Independent Scotland', White Paper, available at http://www.gov.scot/Publications/2013/11/9348.

Scottish National Party, 2011. 'Re-Elect a Scottish Government Working for Scotland', manifesto for the Scottish Parliament elections, available at https://issuu.com/ewanmcintosh/docs/snp_manifesto_2011.

Scottish Parliament, 2007. 'Meeting of the Parliament, Session 3, 16 May', available at http://www.scottish.parliament.uk/parliamentarybusiness/report.aspx?r=4723&mode=pdf.

Scottish Parliamentary Corporate Body, 1999. 'RP 99–17: The Act
    of Settlement', Scottish Parliament Research Briefings, 14 Decem-
    ber, available at http://www.scottishcorpus.ac.uk/document/
    ?documentid=1245.

Seawright, D. and Curtice, J., 1995. 'The decline of the Scottish
    Conservative and Unionist Party 1950–92: Religion, ideology or
    economics?', *Contemporary British History*, 9(2), 319–42.

Seligman, M. E., 1998. *Learned Optimism: How to Change Your Mind
    and Your Life*, New York: Vintage.

Sniderman, P. M., 2000. 'Taking sides: A fixed choice theory of politi-
    cal reasoning', in Lupia, A., McCubbins, M. D., and Popkin, S. L.
    (eds), *Elements of Reason: Cognition, Choice and the Bounds of
    Rationality*, Cambridge: Cambridge University Press.

What Scotland Thinks, 2015. 'Poll of Polls: Westminster Vote Intentions:
    6 May Final', available from http://blog.whatscotlandthinks.
    org/2015/05/poll-of-polls-westminster-vote-intentions-6-may-final.

Widfeldt, A., 1995. 'Party membership and party representativeness',
    in Klingemann, H. D. and Fuchs, D. (eds), *Citizens and the State*,
    Oxford: Oxford University Press.

Wilson, G., 2009. *SNP: The Turbulent Years, 1960–1990*, Stirling: Scots
    Independent Newspapers.

INDEX